AGING WELL

William A. Haseltine
& Jean Galiana

AGING WELL

Solutions to the Most Pressing Global Challenges of Aging

GREENLEAF
BOOK GROUP PRESS

This book is intended as a reference volume only, not as a medical manual. The information given here is designed to help you make informed decisions about your health. It is not intended as a substitute for any treatment that may have been prescribed by your doctor. If you suspect that you have a medical problem, you should seek competent medical help. You should not begin a new health regimen without first consulting a medical professional.

Published by Greenleaf Book Group Press
Austin, Texas
www.gbgpress.com

Previously published by Palgrave Macmillan, 2019, Singapore, 978-981-13-2163-4

Distributed by Greenleaf Book Group

For ordering information or special discounts for bulk purchases, please contact Greenleaf Book Group at PO Box 91869, Austin, TX 78709, 512.891.6100.

Design and composition by Greenleaf Book Group
Cover design by Greenleaf Book Group
Cover illustration: Halfpoint

Publisher's Cataloging-in-Publication data is available.

Print ISBN: 978-1-62634-695-6

eBook ISBN: 978-1-62634-696-3

Part of the Tree Neutral® program, which offsets the number of trees consumed in the production and printing of this book by taking proactive steps, such as planting trees in direct proportion to the number of trees used: www.treeneutral.com

TreeNeutral

Printed in the United States of America on acid-free paper

19 20 21 22 23 24 25   10 9 8 7 6 5 4 3 2 1

Paperback Edition

Contents

List of Figures

Preface

This book is a product of ACCESS Health International (www. accessh.org). ACCESS Health is a think tank, advisory group, and implementation partner dedicated to ensuring that everyone, no matter where they live and no matter what their age, has access to high-quality affordable health care. ACCESS Health works in low-, middle-, and high-income countries. In high-income countries, our focus is on the care of older adults and those with dementia. This book identifies and analyzes policies and practices in the United States that serve as models of excellence in elder care and optimal aging. We chose the title *Aging Well* because we believe that well-being should be the number one focus of all aging care, supports, and interventions. A companion book *Aging with Dignity* examines similar topics in Sweden and several Northern European countries.

Our method was to identify organizations in the United States that exemplify the best in elder care and optimal aging. We then interviewed the leaders and champions of those organizations and programs. The full text of the interviews is available on the ACCESS Health website or at this link: www.accessh.org/agingwell. Here, we analyze our findings and present them in the broader context of elder and dementia care and social inclusion. Our focus areas include long-term care financing, person-centered care, coordinated primary care, home-based palliative and primary care, support for those living with dementia and their caregivers, acute and emergency care in the home and community, the combination of health and social care that addresses the social determinants of health, and housing, social inclusion, purpose, and lifelong learning.

From these interviews we extract eight key lessons for achieving high-quality affordable elder care and effective systems that support social inclusion and purposeful aging. Those lessons are:

- The availability of affordable long-term care insurance is essential to improve access and sustain the costs of caring for older adults.
- Person-centered care is a lynchpin of high-quality care and well-being for older adults.
- Support and palliative care in the home and community setting are essential for making care accessible to older adults that honors their care and late-life priorities.
- Coordinated primary health care improves elder care quality and accessibility and lowers healthcare costs.
- It is imperative that we build systems of support and inclusion for those with dementia and their caregivers.
- Delivery of acute and hospital-level care in the home and community is essential to lower healthcare costs and improve access, health outcomes, and well-being for older adults.
- Social inclusion and the opportunity to live a purposeful life are essential to the happiness and well-being of older adults.
- Combining health and social care with upstream interventions to treat the biopsychosocial and environmental needs is the way forward to sustainable systems of care that improve function, well-being, and independence.

The book identifies and details global aging challenges and, chapter by chapter, offers innovative and impactful solutions to those challenges that our interviewees have designed. It is our genuine hope that providers and government entities around the globe that are seeking methods to improve their elder care and social support systems will find ideas, inspiration, and possibly collaborative opportunities to enhance the well-being of older adults.

New York, New York   William A. Haseltine
Los Angeles, California   Jean Galiana
July 2017

Acknowledgments

We thank all those who contributed their time and thought to help us understand the issues facing older adults and what can be done to ensure that all have access to high-quality affordable care and the opportunity to live productive and active lives.

Claude Thau patiently described the rocky history of the long-term care insurance industry and why many still do not have long-term care insurance today.

We learned the true meaning of patient-centered care culture from Christopher Perna, the former CEO and President of the Eden Alternative. Rebecca Priest from St. John's explained how to build an operational culture around person-centered philosophies.

The leadership of Beatitudes Campus brought the person-centered concept to a new light with their Comfort Matters™ palliative care for those living with dementia.

Dr. Allen Power made us think about the possibility of not segregating those who have dementia from the rest of the community.

They all convinced us that person-centered communication and care is almost always a better option than the use of antipsychotic medications to meet the needs of someone living with dementia.

Dr. Allan Teel of Full Circle America, Dr. Diane E. Meier of the Center to Advance Palliative Care, and Dr. Kristofer Smith of Northwell Health inspired us with their dedication to enabling aging in place and where patients receive the right care in the right setting and live with dignity throughout their life.

Kristofer and Allan have been making house calls throughout their careers because they know that it improves access to care, costs less, and significantly contributes to the well-being of their patients.

Allan connects his patients to local supports and services so that his patients stay engaged and connected to their neighborhoods.

Diane remains vigilant in her pursuit to make palliative care available in all care settings.

Drs. Michael Barr and Erin Giovannetti of the National Committee for Quality Assurance gave us a compelling case for the patient-centered medical home to improve coordinated efficient primary care.

The Director of the James J. Peters VA Medical Center, Dr. Erik Langhoff, uses technology to improve access to high-quality care for veterans.

Dr. Mark Prather and Kevin Riddleberger with DispatchHealth and Dr. Kristofer Smith with Northwell Health are proof positive that delivering acute medical care in the home and community improves access and quality at a fraction of the cost.

Dr. Bruce Leff with Johns Hopkins School of Medicine showed us that providing hospital-level care in the home to patients who qualify can reduce care costs and produce higher-quality health outcomes.

Timothy Peck, Garrett Gleeson, and XiaoSong Mu with Call9 are contributing to the well-being of patients living in skilled nursing by providing technology-enabled emergency care and palliative care around the clock.

Dr. Mary Mittelman with the NYU Caregiver Intervention has proven the value of supporting the informal caregiver for someone living with dementia.

Jed Levine and Elizabeth Santiago tirelessly support those in the early stages of dementia and their caregivers with their vigorous programs at CaringKind.

Davina Porock impressed upon us the importance of the built environment of the hospital for those living with dementia.

Karen Love and Jackie and Lon Pinkowitz remind us of the vital importance of fighting the stigma of dementia with thoughtful community conversations. They also noted the importance of involving those with dementia in policy and program design.

Brian LeBlanc shared his journey of living with dementia and his stories about his impactful advocacy efforts.

June Simmons with the Partners in Care Foundation impressed upon us the need to combine social care and health care and address social determinants of health through evidence-based prevention programs.

Sarah Szanton with CAPABLE proved that it is possible to improve function in frail older adults by providing home modifications with nursing and occupational care to support the goals and priorities of participants.

Joani Blank invited us into her home at the Swan's Market cohousing community in Oakland, California. We spent a half-day seeing how cohousing promotes community inclusion and multigenerational connections.

Rebecca Priest with St. John's and the management of Beatitudes Campus regaled us with stories of resident-run activities that facilitate productive living and generativity.

Anne Doyle surprised us with the amount of lifelong learning and intergenerational connections taking place at Lasell Village, a retirement community on the campus of a college.

Mia Oberlink, formerly with the Center for Home Care Policy and Research, impressed the importance of involving older adults in the design of all initiatives that serve them. Ruth Finkelstein, formerly with the Robert N. Butler Columbia Aging Center and the International

Longevity Center USA, is committed to ensuring that employers who retain and attract older employees are honored so others will follow suit. Ruth and Dorian Block are combating the stigma of aging by telling the stories of older adults who exceeded life expectancy in New York City and are living vibrant productive lives.

Lindsay Goldman with Age-Friendly NYC expressed the need for public and private partnerships to make environments accessible to those of all ages and abilities. She explained that older adults must be considered in all areas of city planning and policy making.

Emi Kiyota showed us how multigenerational community hubs contribute to resilience after natural disasters and serve as places of productive engagement and social inclusion.

Dr. Paul Tang, formerly the Director of the David Druker Center for Health Systems Innovation, uses social connections as a form of health prevention by connecting patients to a timebank where they exchange tasks and teaching of hobbies and new skills.

Our research was supported by the William A. Haseltine Charitable Foundation Trust.

About ACCESS Health International

ACCESS Health International is an independent, nonprofit think tank that works for the provision of high-quality, affordable care for all, including the chronically ill. Our method is to identify, analyze, and document best practices in helping people and to consult with public and private providers to help implement new and better cost-effective ways to offer care. We also encourage entrepreneurs to create new businesses to serve the needs of this rapidly expanding population. Our goal is to inspire and guide healthcare professionals and legislative leaders in all countries to improve care for their own people.

1

Demographics

The commitment of ACCESS Health International to elder care and optimal aging is fueled by the global change in demographics. The population over 60 is expected to double to 22 percent, reaching 2.1 billion from 2000 to 2050.[1] The demographic shift is attributed to increased life span, lower mortality rates, declining immigration rates, and lower fertility rates. Figure 1.1 is an example of the rectangularization process from 1970 to 2060.

The 100-year shift that began in 1950 is only 19 years past its midpoint.[2] By 2060, the pyramid will resemble a dome shape. Some predict that it will morph into the shape of a rectangle[3] because, in many countries, the oldest old (85+) population is growing the fastest.[4] The global population of those 85–99 is projected to increase by 151 percent from 2005 to 2030, while the population of those 100+ is expected to increase by more than 400 percent.[5]

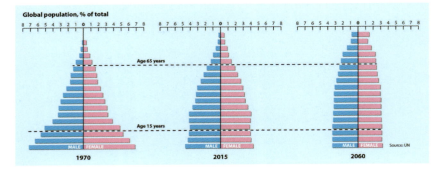

Fig. 1.1 Rectangularization of the global aging pyramid from 1970 to 2060

Table 1.1 Projected global population increase by age group 2005-2030

Age	Percent increase %
0-64	21
65+	104
85+	151
100+	>400

The demographic shift is occurring at varying rates throughout the world (Fig. 1.2). The United Nations reported that, in 2015, almost 25 percent of the world's population 60 and over lived in China and that only four other countries accounted for another 25 percent, including the United States, Japan, India, and the Russian Federation.[6] The projected growth rate for the over 60 population also varies from country to country, but is expected to continue to grow globally until 2060.

Potential Support Ratio

One result of the demographic shift is that there will be substantially more older people who need care and fewer younger people to provide the care. This care conundrum is reflected in the potential support ratio—the number of workers (age 15–65) to the number of retirees (65+). The potential support ratio has been declining substantially from 2000 to 2050 (Fig. 1.3).

Percentage of Population Aged 65 and Over: 2015 and 2050

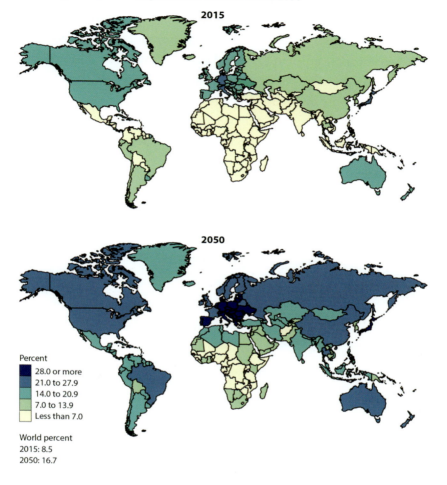

Fig. 1.2 Global distribution of population 65 and over in 2015 and 2050. Source: US Census Bureau, 2013, 2014a, 2014b; International Data Base, US population estimates, and US population projections

With the shrinking potential support ratio, who will care for the growing number of older adults? Immigration is one answer, but the overarching response should be that health care and social support systems become more efficient to meet the significant needs of this cohort. Informal caregivers make invaluable contributions, but they cannot meet the complex care needs of the growing older population. This care gap is further magnified when considering the rates of comorbidity and cognitive and functional limitations of the older population.

Potential support ratios by region, 2015, 2030 and 2050

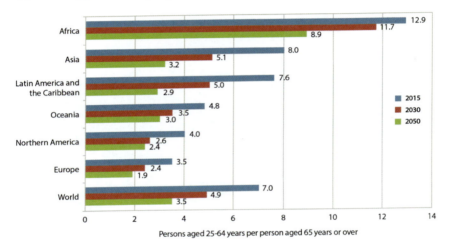

Fig. 1.3 Potential support ratios by region, 2015, 2030, and 2050. Source: UN Department of Economic and Social Affairs

We will begin with some facts about health care in the United States and then describe solutions to the challenges we have laid out.

2

Health Care in the United States

United States Health Spending and Outcomes

The health spending of the United States is the highest among the Organisation for Economic Co-operation and Development (OECD) countries. It was 2.5 times greater than the OECD average in 2013.[1] Health spending accounted for 16.4 percent of the gross domestic product in 2013[2] and, in 2020, it is projected to represent 20 percent.[3] By 2040 it is estimated that one third of all spending in the US will be on health care.[4,5] Despite all of the spending, the health of Americans lags behind. This is, in large part, a result of America divesting from prevention and health promotion programs. Another contributing factor to such poor health outcomes is that the US does not invest enough in building robust systems of primary care.[6] Although the US spends close to the same amount as other Western countries on health care and social supports combined, it spends proportionately less on social services and more on health care to treat people after they become ill[7] from what are often preventable diseases. Adults in the US are more likely than adults in other developed nations to forgo necessary health care because they cannot afford the cost.[8] From 2010 to 2012, 54 percent of people with chronic illness reported that cost was a barrier for them to access care. The patients surveyed reported that they skipped medications, treatments, and doctor visits because they could not afford the cost.[9] Life expectancy is shorter in the US than most OECD countries. As of 2013 life expectancy in the US was 78.8, while the OECD average was 80.5.[10] In 2014 the Commonwealth Fund ranked the United States health care last among 11 countries.[11,12] The measures included access, equity, quality, efficiency, and healthy lives. Because of these findings, the government and many health systems in the US are creating new care models to address the issues of healthcare access, quality (including patient satisfaction), and cost. Many of these innovations are designed to serve older adults because the older cohort interacts with the healthcare system more than others.

Our ultimate goal, after all, is not a good death but a good life to the very end. (Atul Gawande, *Being Mortal: Medicine and What Matters in the End*)

Optimal Aging

In the US and internationally, there is a continuing focus on community supports and inclusive societies that allow older adults to remain active and engaged. This focus includes age-friendly cities, inclusive housing, and employment opportunities. Most of the improvement in health care and inclusive environments will positively affect those with dementia, but providers and city planners are also committed to implementing dementia-specific care and support measures.

Geriatric Workforce Shortage

Geriatricians are a critical factor of high-quality care for older adults. The US is already struggling with the ability to care for the older population with the high rates of dementia and other chronic illnesses and is lacking in a workforce with appropriate training.[13] According to the American Geriatrics Society, as of 2015, the US was short 9,500 geriatricians.[14] This shortage threatens to grow as the population ages. The World Health Organization cites that to meet the need of the growing older population, all healthcare providers must be educated in gerontology and geriatrics.[15] Some suggest that having more geriatricians in the hospital setting could reduce costs.[16] This is important because 25 percent of Medicare spending is attributable to inpatient hospital care.[17] Geriatricians are trained to understand and diagnose cognitive problems and functional challenges with activities of daily living. They also are knowledgeable about how drugs act differently in the aging body and are adept at polypharmacy management. Additionally, geriatricians are trained to manage multiple comorbidities and understand that health management is often the primary focus rather than cure.

Prevalence of Chronic Disease

Longevity and lifestyle choices such as smoking, alcohol, and obesity have contributed to people developing more chronic illnesses. The occurrence of multiple chronic conditions increases with age,[18] which compounds the burden of caring for the growing aging population. Almost one half of older adults in America are living with both chronic conditions and functional limitations.[19] Eighty percent have at least one chronic condition, and 50 percent have at least two.[20] Approximately 75 percent of Americans 65 and older are living with multiple chronic conditions[21] and 20 percent are living with five or more chronic conditions.[22] The oldest old population (80 and older) is growing most rapidly[23, 24] and has the highest rates of comorbidity.

The number of people living with dementia is projected to increase by more than 200 percent, from 44 million in 2014 to 135 million by 2050.[25] One in nine people 65 and older has dementia. The statistics, however, do not accurately represent the prevalence of dementia because an estimated 50 to 90 percent of dementia cases go undiagnosed.[26,27] The global average rate of undiagnosed cases of dementia is 75 percent.[28] The rates of undiagnosed dementia vary from country to country. The highest rates are found in the low- and middle-income countries.[29] It is nearly impossible to separate elder care from dementia care after the age of 75 because that population represents 81 percent of the cases of dementia.[30] As we mentioned, the oldest old is the population that is growing the fastest. Thirty-two percent of that cohort have received a diagnosis of dementia.[31]

It is more expensive to meet the complex care needs of people with multiple chronic conditions. Many will also need supportive help because those with multiple chronic conditions experience higher levels of poor functional status.[32,33] Older adults who are living with five or more chronic illnesses have, on average, 50 prescriptions and 14 different physicians and make 37 office visits annually.[34] Those with multiple chronic conditions account for 71 percent of the total health care spending in the United States.[35] The fee-for-service individuals with multiple chronic conditions, who are beneficiaries of the government-sponsored Medicare, accounts for 93 percent of the total Medicare spending.[36] The unsustainability of medical costs is an incentive for the Centers for Medicare and Medicaid Services to support more efficient, less costly, and better quality systems of care for the sickest people. The financial burden is also borne by people living with multiple chronic conditions through out-of-pocket costs and the high price of prescription medications.

Meeting the healthcare and social needs of the older population is a worldwide public health challenge. To properly and sustainably meet the needs of older adults, providers must challenge fragmented and complex care and social support systems and implement coordinated, person-centered care across a variety of care settings and providers. Providers must also foster chronic disease self-management programs and other forms of patient engagement. Two important concepts that we address throughout the book that serve to promote higher-quality accessible care with greater patient satisfaction at a lower cost are person-centered and value-based care.

Person-Centered Care

One theme that occurs throughout our interviews involving elder care is the concept of person-centered care.[37] Rather than being provider led, person-centered care has the patient in the center of the care team with all care decisions based around the goals and priorities of the patient. Person-centered care has been the focus of global health systems and policy makers.[38,39] Although beneficial for everyone, person-centered care is especially effective in treating those who are most frail and living with multiple chronic conditions. Person-centered care has the potential to lower the health system utilization of the patient by providing more coordinated care and better self-management support that helps keep patients out of the emergency departments and hospitals.

Person-centered care providers have discussions with their patients about the benefits and side effects of aggressive interventions. They involve the patient and their families in care planning, including advanced directives for late life. In the last years of life, often people who are involved in their care planning will opt out of heroic medical interventions and enjoy life in the way they most prefer. Person-centered care is value-based care because it improves quality of life, reduces healthcare utilization, and lowers the care cost in late life.[40,41,42,43]

Value-Based Care

Value is measured as the ratio of health cost and outcomes. The goal of value-based care is to lower health spending by reducing redundancies and unnecessary care. In a fee-for-service reimbursement arrangement, providers are paid for each service they perform, including office visits, tests, operations, and other medical procedures. The more volume, the more the provider makes, which can be seen as an incentive for too much care. Unnecessary medical tests and procedures cost the American healthcare system an estimated US$200 billion each year and overly aggressive care is responsible for an estimated 30,000 deaths annually.[44] Since the passage of the Affordable Care Act in 2010 and the Medicare and CHIP Reauthorization Act (MACRA) of 2015, the United States has been in the process of a historic change in the way health care is reimbursed. Healthcare providers are reorganizing how they deliver care in the response to reimbursements that incentivize value over volume.

The Centers for Medicare and Medicaid Services, private payers, fully integrated health systems such as managed care organizations, and large employers have led the push toward value-based reimbursement policy. They have built in incentives to provide value because they exist as the payer and the payee of health services. Private insurers including Aetna and Blue Cross Blue Shield are dedicating an increasing amount of their spending toward value-based care.[45] Large employers such as Intel, Starbucks,[46] Boeing, General Electric, Lowe's, and Walmart[47] have forged their own way to value-based care by negotiating with insurers and medical providers to receive better quality care at a lower cost.

Value care arrangements shift health systems from a medical model to a public health model. There are a variety of value-based reimbursement arrangements or alternate payment models.

SHARED SAVINGS

The provider is given an agreed upon fee that is based on the health profile of the patient. If the provider is able to meet specified outcome benchmarks at a lower cost, that savings is kept by the provider or shared at a predetermined rate with the insurer.

SHARED RISK

If the organization spends more than the agreed upon amount, they are required to repay the insurer for some of the excess spending.

BUNDLED PAYMENTS

The insurer makes one payment for the total care linked to a particular procedure or period of time. This fee covers the cost of care across the continuum. If an organization is efficient and does not spend the total fee they received, they can keep the savings. The Centers for Medicare and Medicaid Services have made bundled payments mandatory for heart attack treatment, bypass surgery, hip and knee replacement, and surgical hip and femur fracture treatment.[48]

GLOBAL CAPITATION

Insurers pay a set monthly fee for each patient. The fee is meant to pay for all of the healthcare services used by the patient.

PAY FOR PERFORMANCE

The provider is compensated based on the evaluation of the physician performance metrics. Those who meet the targets established by the insurer may receive a bonus.

Value-based agreements encourage providers to be committed to coordinated, high-quality care because a trip to the emergency department, complications resulting from medication mismanagement, a readmission after a care transition, and other often preventable adverse health events can increase the cost of care substantially. The agreements also give providers more flexibility in resource allocation. Value-based agreements have set the stage for better care in all settings, including the home and community. With the new president, the US is unsure of future healthcare reimbursement policies, but it is doubtful that we will move away from value-based care. Like the US, all countries who are aligning their healthcare systems and policies to meet the needs of their growing older population will need to maintain a vigilant dedication to value-based care and health system redesign.

Alignment to Meet the Needs of the Older Population

The increase in life expectancy is a public health success, and possibly the greatest achievement of the twentieth century. However, the challenge remains for health systems, private entities, and policy makers, from the community level through the federal level, to ensure that people can live the highest quality of life possible (optimal aging) in their additional years. Optimal aging is not solely about health status; it is being able to live active, engaged, and productive lives due to policies and practices that foster inclusive communities for people of all ages and abilities. This public health challenge presents unprecedented opportunities for innovation and we are pleased to share some of our favorites in the following pages.

This is a book of solutions to some of the most pressing challenges in aging today.

In the following chapters, we will describe organizational cultures of elder care providers that are person-centered, coordinated, and efficient and, therefore, require fewer staff and result in better health outcomes, improved access, and lower care costs. We will also detail innovations that support people with dementia and their caregivers that enable those with dementia to remain safely at home and included in their communities. We will show how some models of care have greatly reduced costs and improved outcomes by providing care in the home and community, while others combine social and health supports to improve function and enable aging in place. We will also present models of illness and injury prevention and chronic disease self-management that reduce healthcare utilization greatly and improve the well-being of older adults. We will begin with long-term care financing and why the long-term care industry is less than vibrant in the US. The next chapter makes a convincing case for the need for universal health coverage to meet the growing global long-term care needs of the aging population.

3

Long-Term Care Financing

An estimated 12 million people in the United States currently need long-term care.[1] In the US, long-term care is often referred to as long-term services and supports (LTSS), which include health care and assistance with activities of daily living (ADLs).[2] Some common services and supports include caregiver assistance, nursing home care, adult day care, home health and personal assistance, and transportation. By 2050, the number of those needing long-term care is projected to more than double to 27 million[3] (Fig. 3.1). Nearly 70 percent of those 65 and older will need some form of long-term care in their lifetime,[4] and 20 percent will need it for five or more years.[5] The annual cost of long-term care today is approximately US$725 billion.[6] As the population continues to age, healthcare costs could potentially reach unsustainable levels. Medicaid estimates that their spending on LTSS will increase six percent annually through 2021.[7] When the baby boom generation[8] begins to reach age 85 in 2030, the spending growth for LTSS will be further accelerated and will represent three percent of the GDP by 2050.[9]

The percentage of GDP of public long-term care expenditures of the OECD countries is projected to grow from 0.8 in 2010 to 1.6 in 2060. For the BRIICS countries (Brazil, Russia, India, Indonesia, China, and South Africa), the growth projection of long-term care expenditures is from 0.1 to 0.9 percent of GDP.[10]

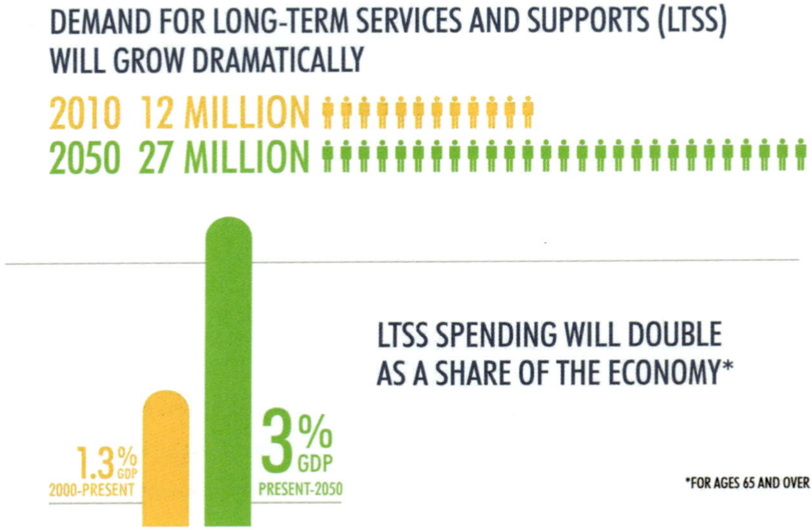

DEMAND FOR LONG-TERM SERVICES AND SUPPORTS (LTSS) WILL GROW DRAMATICALLY

2010   12 MILLION ††††††††††††
2050   27 MILLION ††††††††††††††††††††††††††††††

LTSS SPENDING WILL DOUBLE AS A SHARE OF THE ECONOMY*

1.3% GDP
2000-PRESENT

3% GDP
PRESENT-2050

*FOR AGES 65 AND OVER

Fig 3.1 Growth in demand for LTSS. Source: Bipartisan Policy Center

Managed care and home-based care are two trends that can lower costs and improve care. Government-funded Medicaid contracts with managed care organizations and pays a monthly capitated payment per patient. As described in Chap. 1, this value-based care reimbursement arrangement is an incentive for healthcare systems to be efficiently integrated and provide higher-quality, lower-cost care. As mentioned previously, in an effort to lower costs and improve quality of life for older patients, health providers are moving toward person-centered home-based models and away from institutional care. This trend is also taking place globally. Other housing models that can contribute to lower LTSS costs are neighborhoods such as villages (V2V) and naturally occurring retirement communities (NORCs), where residents receive care and support collectively. We will describe these housing models in Chap. 7.

Even with better emerging delivery and reimbursement models, health systems around the world are facing challenges in financing higher quality, lower-cost long-term services and supports for their older citizens.

Global Funding Goals

The global demographic shift indicates that many nations around the world are faced with the pressing need of financially sustainable health systems to provide long-term care. Lower- and middle-income countries are less prepared to address the need. Global data regarding the lack of access to long-term care exists only on a national level, and according to the World Health Organization, data reveal large gaps in the provision of and access to such services in many low- and middle-income countries.[11]

AARP (formerly the American Association of Retired Persons) distilled the common goals of developed countries with differing models of long-term care financing and health and service delivery that include:[12]

- Providing "consumer-directed" home care and programs to enhance choice and independence;
- Encouraging home and community-based services rather than institutional care;
- Encouraging family support of persons with disabilities;
- Providing universal coverage for long-term care services;
- Insuring individuals against the high costs of long-term care through a mix of public and private financing;
- Improving the coordination between chronic medical care and long-term care services.

Barriers to Sustainable Long-Term Care Financing in the United States

PUBLIC KNOWLEDGE

Most Americans do not know how the long-term care system operates. As a result, they do not support financing reforms that would make supporting long-term care possible.[13] The citizens of the US must be educated about the existing long-term care system or the much-needed reform will not happen. Lack of knowledge of the long-term care system, along with denial, leaves many unprepared for the costs that they will likely incur in old age.

> Long-term care expenses are one of the greater economic risks that older Americans face. (Richard Johnson, former director, Urban Institute, Program on Retirement Policy)[14]

Cost

Not everyone can afford private long-term care insurance. The annual cost of a policy for a couple at age 55 can range from US$2,085 to US$3,970, depending on the insurer, the policy purchased, and health profile of the purchaser.[15] Long-term care insurance has inherent risks to the policyholder who may not be able to continue paying every year. When beneficiaries let their policies lapse, the annual premiums that they may have paid for decades are lost, and will not be available to pay for their future care.

Reimbursement Policy

Medicare and private insurers do not reimburse for long-term nursing home stays. In 2016, the average annual cost of nursing home care ranged from approximately US$82,128 for a semi-private room to US$92,376 for a private room.[16] On average, people will need three years of long-term care in their lifetime.[17] The beneficiaries will also realize high out-of-pocket expenses related to long-term care. These costs are not affordable by most.[18] Many are forced to spend down their savings and sell their homes.

Only after a person has depleted almost all of their savings will they be eligible for long-term care reimbursement from Medicaid. Medicaid is a means and/or disability tested, joint federal and state government financed healthcare insurance that covers home care, assisted living, and skilled nursing care. The process of obtaining Medicaid at this stage is complicated and difficult for older individuals to navigate. Additionally, asset depletion can leave a surviving spouse and or family in financial ruin.

Another option for lower-income families is to keep the older relative at home and become the informal caregiver. This option places physical and emotional strain on the caregiver, who is most often an older female living with health challenges of her own. Many countries have recognized the integral role of the informal caregiver in enabling a person to remain at home and the considerable financial value this care brings to the health system. Recognition has come in the form of paid leave (care leave), respite support,[19] and financial reimbursement.

Veterans in the US receive a pension and some support with home care and assisted living. The combination makes long-term care affordable by most veterans but not without out-of-pocket costs.

Long-Term Care Insurance

With the present and rapidly growing need for long-term care, one would expect that the long-term care insurance industry in the US would be thriving. In his interview, insurance expert Claude Thau reveals that it is anything but.

CLAUDE THAU
THAU INCORPORATED

Claude Thau is the president of Thau Incorporated, which provides consulting services to insurers, employers, regulators, and businesses that offer services to the long-term care insurance industry.

It would be tempting to assume that the long-term care insurance industry is suffering due to the fact that Americans are living longer with higher rates of comorbidity, healthcare costs are rising, and the cost of medications are skyrocketing. Surprisingly, these are not the main reasons the industry is struggling.

In the 1980s, many insurers in the US began to offer private long-term policies. It was a new product for insurers and they did not have adequate data to accurately calculate risk. Claude explained that the two most critical measures of risk factors were interest rates and lapse rates.

No one could have possibly anticipated the investment income yield climates we have experienced in the past decade.

When insurers receive premium payments, they place those funds in interest earning accounts. Most of the money insurers use to pay long-term care claims comes from the interest earned because insurers set aside large reserves (to remain solvent) for a long time in support of long-term care insurance policies. In the mid to late 1990s, actuaries were assuming that these accounts would earn seven percent net income. Interest rates in the US dropped to historic lows, causing insurers to be short by three to four percent annually. The low insurance rates dealt a powerful blow to long-term care insurers, but the unpredictably low lapse rate caused an even bigger problem.

A one percent difference in lapse rate hurts profits as much as a one percent reduction in investment income.

When an insured person does not continue to pay their premiums, their policy lapses. When the policy lapses, all of the reserve that the insurance company has set aside over the years can be released. The insurer accumulated payments, but will not bear the responsibility of paying for expensive long-term care for the person whose policy lapsed. The released reserves can be used to pay for future claims of policyholders who kept up to date with their premium payments or become profit.

If, when determining the price for long-term care insurance, insurers ignored the possibility that people would let their policies lapse, the prices would be higher and the insurers would reap large benefits when policies lapsed. To avoid that situation and provide a better deal to consumers, insurers reflect expected lapses when pricing policies.

In the mid-1990s, reinsurers, companies that insure insurance companies, recommended that insurers assume an eight percent lapse rate each year after the first two years a policy was in place. This was a fateful recommendation. The actual lapse rate was seven tenths of a percent, leaving insurers with the responsibility of paying for many more beneficiaries than they had anticipated. By 2010, insurers had four times as many policies in effect than they had predicted. This dramatically increased the amount of claims insurers had to reimburse. Claude explained that the higher priced policies of today are adjusted to assume a more accurate interest and lapse rate prediction.

Based on our research, we believe current policies are too expensive for many individuals. This highlights the need for individual, public, and private involvement to advocate for financing policy that includes universal health coverage for the millions of Americans who will need long-term care. In this arena, America has a lot to learn from other developed countries.

In our next chapter, we write about long-term care that is person-centered and organizationally efficient. The methods and models are a glimmer of hope for the possibility of reducing long-term care costs and improving health outcomes and quality of life for those living in long-term care residences.

The full interview of Claude Thau can be found at this link: www. accessh.org/agingwell.

4

Person-Centered Long-Term Care

The number of older adults in the world in need of long-term care is expected to reach 277 million by 2050.[1] In 2014, approximately nine million people in the United States received long-term care services from adult day care programs, home health agencies, hospice organizations, nursing homes, and senior living communities.[2] As of July 2014, there were 15,600 long-term care residences that were home to 1.4 million people.[3] The number of people needing long-term care will continue to grow as the aging population increases and people live longer with more chronic conditions and cognitive and functional limitations. From 2000 to 2050, the number of people in need of long-term care is projected to more than double from 13 to 27 million.[4]

Person-Centered Long-Term Care

Long-term care organizations are moving away from a traditional model of care to what is referred to as person-centered or person-directed care. Thomas Kitwood, a psychologist from the United Kingdom, spearheaded this movement approximately 20 years ago.[5] The traditional long-term care model takes a more standardized, institutional, medical approach with top-down decision making inherent in a vertical organizational culture. Person-centered care uses an interpersonal approach that is steeped in the philosophies of dignity, comfort, well-being, and respect. Person-centered is a shift from a culture where the provider and staff dictate when people will sleep, eat, and shower; what they will eat; and what they will do for activities to honoring the individual rhythms and preferences of the patient. In a person-centered culture, the staff acts as a single team that shares responsibilities and accountability. The staff is empowered to be part of the system design and care planning and to form meaningful connected relationships with the residents.

Throughout a culture change, hierarchy begins to flatten and decision making moves closer and closer to the elders and their care teams—no matter where the elders live.
(Christopher Perna)

The person and the family are in the center of the person-directed care organizational structure and are part of every decision regarding their care and daily routine. This enables and encourages elders to communicate what is most important to them in their life and in their death and what should be prioritized to meet those wishes. Some of our interviewees, such as the leadership of Beatitudes Campus, would describe meeting the psychological, physical, and spiritual needs of their residents as providing comfort. Others, like Christopher Perna, Dr. Allen Power, and Rebecca Priest, who embrace the Eden Alternative philosophies, may refer to the same as enabling well-being. The person-centered paradigm shift has been described as the provider moving away from thinking, "What is the matter?" to "What matters to our patients?"[6] A person-centered model of care is not limited to the long-term care, memory care, or assisted living settings. Formal and informal caregivers of a person living at home and staff of adult day care centers can adopt person-centered philosophies and practices.

The built environment can support person-directed care. The small home setting promotes a nurturing environment where 10–20 residents live. The Green House Project,[7] founded by Jude and Bill Thomas,[8] led the small home movement in the US. Components of a small home that contribute to well-being or comfort include private bedrooms, beds that are not hospital beds and do not have side rails, gentle lighting, large communal living spaces, no alarms, plants, and often animals. Life and living are central to the homes with the great room, the kitchen, and the dining room in the center of the house. The homes have the same care team each day and the team shares responsibilities much in the way family members would. The business case for the small home person-centered model is convincing. The Green House Project model realizes better financial outcomes than traditional models of long-term care. Green House providers have witnessed 7 percent higher occupancy rates, 24 percent private pay occupancy, equal or less in capital costs, and equal staffing costs.[9] We will describe other financial benefits of person-centered long-term care throughout the chapter.

Researchers at the LeadingAge Center for Applied Research are conducting an ongoing study of culture change in the long-term care setting.[10] They have found that a fully implemented person-centered culture change resulted in residents experiencing improved perceptions of their quality of life. Other outcomes included reductions in:

- Depressive symptoms;
- Antipsychotic drug use;
- Pressure ulcers;

- Incontinence episodes;
- Catheter use; and
- Urinary tract infections.

Our interviewees have realized similar outcomes. In the subsequent interview summaries you will find reoccurring themes of the person-centered care design and operation. Some of the themes are the patient and family as an integral part of the decision-making care team, individualized daily life for the patients, smaller home-like settings, behavior as communication for those living with dementia, continued education and adaptation, and staff that does not rotate.

Dr. Thomas began to envision a culture of care where people can thrive, not just survive. (Christopher Perna)

CHRISTOPHER PERNA
THE EDEN ALTERNATIVE®

Christopher Perna is the former President and CEO of the Eden Alternative. Jude Thomas and Harvard-trained geriatrician Dr. William Thomas founded the Eden Alternative in 1990 as a response to nursing homes that were too harsh and medical. They set out to reimagine long-term care in a home-like setting with plants, animals, and a team of caring professionals who behave, in many ways, like family. They identified three main issues or plagues facing those living in long-term care: the plagues of loneliness, helplessness, and boredom. Inspiration to address the three plagues led to the ten founding principles of the Eden Alternative. In 2004, Jude and Bill Thomas convened a task force of culture-change experts and established the seven Domains of Well-being. Those domains are identity, growth, autonomy, security, connectedness, meaning, and joy.

It is not about being politically correct—it is about shifting
how your brain perceives things. (Christopher Perna)

Words Make Worlds

An important aspect of the Eden Alternative culture is the use of words. They believe that words make worlds and choose to use words that are respectful and that speak to a person's abilities rather than disabilities. Some examples include:

- Someone is living with dementia or memory challenges rather than suffering with Alzheimer's.
- The clinical team is referred to as care partners—some even remove the word care from that term.
- Person-centered care is often referred to as person-directed care.
- Patients are referred to as residents.
- Facilities are referred to as homes, residences, or communities.
- Older individuals are referred to as Elders—always with a capital E.

Training and Outcomes of Eden Alternative Adoption

The Eden Alternative trains care professionals to operationalize the patient-centered culture for home, assisted living, skilled nursing, and long-term care residences. They offer a variety of trainings, consulting services, and educational programs, including webinars. Providers can become part of the Eden Alternative Registry by completing training that generally takes 12–18 months. During this process, providers are coached and guided in culture change specific to their organization.

Signature Healthcare[11] is a recognized Eden Alternative provider.

In 2012 they began to implement culture change and operationalize the Eden Alternative philosophies and principles. Today the Signature Hometown[12] arm has 60 residences for older adults that are located in rural communities of six states. Forty of those residences are on the Eden Alternative registry. Signature Healthcare conducted a five-year retrospective review study to measure the impact of their culture transformation.[13] The researchers studied the homes that are on the Eden Alternative registry and used those that are not yet on the registry as control comparisons. The researchers found that homes on the Eden Alternative Registry saw improvements in operational and quality outcomes.

Operational outcomes:

- Higher occupancy rates;
- More monthly admissions to their homes;
- Much higher earnings before interest, tax, depreciation, and amortization;
- Better Center for Medicare and Medicaid Five-Star Quality Ratings;[14]
- Lower rate of nurse turnover; and
- Lower number of worker's compensation claims.

Health outcomes:

- Lower incidence of depressive symptoms;
- Elimination of all incidences of pressure ulcers;
- Substantially lower number of daily medications taken;
- Lowered use of antipsychotic medications;
- Substantially fewer hospital readmissions;

- Fewer residences needing assistance with the activities of daily living;
- Great reduction in the number of falls; and
- Much less weight loss for residents.

Eden Alternative International Regional Coordinators are active in Australia, Austria, Canada, Denmark, the Faroe Islands, Finland, Germany, Iceland, the Netherlands, New Zealand, Norway, South Africa, Sweden, Switzerland, and the United Kingdom. The coordinators are trained and licensed as ambassadors to bring the Eden Alternative training and principles to providers around the world.[15]

REBECCA PRIEST
ST. JOHN'S

Rebecca Priest is the former Administrator of Skilled Nursing at St. John's Home. Rochester, New York-based St. John's is a full-spectrum senior service provider with four home and village-like campuses.

In 2001, with the guidance of Eden Alternative training, Rebecca and her team embarked on the implementation of the Eden Alternative philosophies into their organizational culture. Rebecca, the administrator of skilled nursing, had the full support of the board and the president and CEO Charlie Runyon—support that Rebecca claims was crucial to their success.

We have a built environment with cues to remind the residents that they are in their house. It is not an institutional space that belongs to a medical team. It is the home of the Elders.

Small Homes

Two of St. John's campuses are dedicated to long-term care and are on the Eden Alternative Registry. Both have a small home setting and care culture. The St. John's Home is especially interesting because the structure of the residence is a tall institutional style building. The floors are H shaped with long narrow hallways like a hospital. The building is not how one would envision small homes. Rebecca Priest and her team have creatively renovated and redesigned the floors into small homes that are centered not around the nursing station, but around the living room and dining room of the residents. This is a physical example of placing the Elders in the center of the organizational structure and prioritizing their needs for social connection and a warm home-like environment. The residents bring their own furniture for their rooms and are encouraged to decorate the shared spaces with some of their sentimental items.

St. John's Penfield campus consists of two Green House properties that are home to ten Elders each. These homes are indistinguishable from the others in the residential neighborhood (Fig. 4.1). The homes have the physical characteristics of the Green House design, including a large great room, kitchen, and dining room that are central to the structure. At the time of my visit, the Green Houses had a pet dog and a large garden space that connected the two homes (Fig. 4.2). In her Ted Talk, Rebecca explained that the new model of person-centered care in the small home setting and community has changed the concept of long-term care and opened the door for others to follow suit.[16]

The built environment is useful in sending cues that feel like home, but the culture of the care team is the most important aspect of the Eden Alternative philosophies. One vital component of that culture is a care team that does not rotate (dedicated staff assignment) and knows the individual preferences and needs of the residents. This is beneficial from a quality-of-life perspective because the Elders know the people who are caring for them on a daily basis. The care partners who are helping the Elders, with intimate personal care are not strangers. We will delve into this subject in more depth a little further into this chapter.

Fig. 4.1 Green House at Penfield

Fig. 4.2 Penfield Green House great room

We support an operational structure that allows for innovation and quality assurance from the staff, without blanket policies from the administration.

Care Team Empowerment

The St. John's care partners are an integral part of the design and execution of all of their duties. This empowerment gives them ownership in the process. When care partners behave as a team and share responsibilities and accountability equally, the quality of care is better. The comparison example of a siloed care team Rebecca gave was one in which a resident who had pneumonia or a bad cold had finished eating. After the meal, the care partner would not leave the clean-up for the housekeeping staff. He or she would immediately wipe the area with disinfectant because the resident was ill. If the clean-up was left until the housekeeping staff arrived for their rounds, there would be more chance of contaminating the other residents. The care team is trained in versatility and can meet all the needs of the elders. If one care partner neglects an overflowing wastebasket, another will either bring it to the attention of the care team member or change the basket him or herself. This is much like the way siblings would take care of their older family member. This model has resulted in better safety and cleanliness at St. John's.

When an organization uses this type of team-based culture, they need fewer full-time employees, which creates consistency and deeper connectedness to the residents. It also lowers overhead cost. The staff to resident ratio in the small home person-centered model is 1:4 as compared to the average of traditional skilled nursing facilities in the Rochester region, which is 1:6. At first glance, one might conclude that fewer staff would indicate less time to spend directly with the residents.

The outcomes, however, are in stark contrast with that conclusion. St. John's caregivers provide 45 percent more direct hours per patient daily than the average of regional traditional skilled nursing facilities. The increased caregiver attention has resulted in 80 percent fewer resident falls as compared to the traditional skilled nursing model.

Staff Satisfaction

As experienced by Signature Healthcare, after the Eden Alternative principles were operationalized at St. John's, their caregiver turnover rate plunged. Rebecca attributes this lower turnover rate to the fact that the care partners enjoy their jobs more because they are an empowered part of the team and they establish rewarding relationships with the Elders. Call-ins are when a staff member calls in sick or is otherwise unable to go to work. St. John's receives 75 percent fewer staff call-ins than the regional average of skilled nursing facilities that do not embrace the Eden Alternative principles and the small home model. This is beneficial for consistency and stability with the residents and is financially advantageous because there is less need to train new staff.

Shifting from uniforms to regular attire is one of the stepping stones for culture change.

Uniforms

To promote a less clinical environment Rebecca encourages the care partners to wear casual professional attire in lieu of scrubs or other uniforms. Research has shown that when Elders see people in uniforms, they act sicker and more dependent.[17,18,19,20] Rebecca and her team witnessed their residents behaving more independently when the care team began wearing professional attire. The residents were more likely to try to move out to the garden or go into the kitchen for a snack on their own.

Those with Dementia Live in Community

Most people living in long-term care have dementia.[21] Rebecca estimates that 87 percent of the residents of St. John's long-term care homes have some stage of dementia. It requires refined organizational processes to create a person-directed care environment to meet their needs. The residents of St. John's who have dementia live in community, meaning they are not segregated onto a different floor or building. Rebecca maintains that this is possible because the care partners know the residents individually and can interpret their behaviors. Often those with dementia cannot express their needs accurately with words and will do so through behavior. Many clinicians will react to this behavior with antipsychotic medications and label them as resisting care. A person-centered caregiver would recognize the behavior as an unmet need.

While I was visiting St. John's, I had the pleasure of meeting Mr. H, a resident in the later stages of dementia. I learned that when Mr. H first began living at St. John's, he and the other residents faced some challenges in how they related to each other. The care team wanted to understand Mr. H's needs so they decided to find out more about him. They met with him and his family and compiled a binder about him that is on display and available to the care partners and the other residents. They learned Mr. H was an avid traveler and a marathon runner and concluded that might be why he likes to walk around most of the time. They also made the binder about Mr. H's life so they could have appreciation for his accomplishments and see him through the lens of his abilities rather than his difficulties.

Another behavior of Mr. H caught the eye of the care team. When Mr. H would approach his fellow residents, he would often touch their hair or their arm. People did not know how to react to this somewhat intrusive habit. After further examination, a St. John's dementia specialist decided that his unmet need was that of touch and human connection. Today, whenever the care team greets Mr. H, they offer him a hug, which is uplifting for the care partners and Mr. H. This is one example of the level of person-centered dedication that is required to meet the needs of someone who is living with dementia. This type of intervention has resulted in St. John's seeing a 100 percent decline in adverse elder-to-elder interactions and behaviors.

The residents of St. John's Home have a lot of spaces that foster meaningful connection and autonomy. The multi-storied building has an ice cream shop, a library, comfortable lobbies with fireplaces, a nursery school, and a courtyard. The only locked doors are those that lead outside to the parking lot and streets.

Enabling People to Die in Their Home

The disparity between the number of people who prefer to die at home and the number who actually do die at home is of great interest to providers of person-centered care. Despite the fact that 80 percent of Americans would prefer to die at home, only 20 percent do.[22] The desire to die at home is not unique to the US and neither is the inability of the healthcare system to make it possible.[23] We will cover this subject in more detail in the forthcoming interview summaries of Diane E. Meier and Kristofer Smith. Saint John's is able to provide better end-of-life care than traditional skilled nursing centers because they have a system that is capable of honoring the wishes of the residents. They also involve residents and their families in the care plan, including the advance care directive.[24] In St. John's, 70 percent of the care residents die in their home and 30 percent die in the hospital. These outcomes can be compared to the regional averages of traditional skilled nursing facilities that are not using the small home model. In these facilities, 80 percent of the residents die in the hospital and 20 percent die in the care home.

Stakeholder Satisfaction

The average satisfaction rate for traditional skilled nursing residences in the Rochester region is 74 percent. St. John's has achieved a 100 percent satisfaction rate from residents and their families. They attribute this to their small homecare culture based in the Eden Alternative philosophies (Fig. 4.3).

> Policies that are good for dementia are almost always good for everyone. Good dementia care is good elder care and vice versa.

Antipsychotic Medications

The Centers for Medicare and Medicaid Services and care providers around the world are concerned with the high rate of antipsychotic usage.[25,26] All of the people who first move into St. John's Green House residences and most of those entering St. John's Home are on some form of antipsychotic medication. St. John's welcomes those who have had difficulty adjusting to other long-term care homes. Rebecca and her team use person-centered interventions to meet the needs of the residents rather than medicate their behavior. Mr. H is a perfect example.

Fig. 4.3 St. John's to traditional skilled nursing regional comparison

St. John's also has no alarms except for exceptional circumstances, no glaring lights, no beeping machinery, no blaring televisions, and no overhead or intercom system, because they contribute to a disruptive environment for all of the residents and more so to those who are living with dementia. Because new residents are moving in regularly and some may have mental health issues, the rates of antipsychotic usage are rarely zero. Today St. John's has accomplished a great reduction in the number of residents taking antipsychotic medications. They have a 15 percent rate of antipsychotic usage in both of their care homes: 10 percent in St. John's Home where 450 elders reside and 5 percent in the Green

Houses where a total of 20 people reside. Dr. Allen Power is an Eden Alternative trained geriatrician who was formerly with St. John's. Today he travels the world championing person-directed care and advocating against the use of antipsychotic medications for those with dementia.

> People with dementia are frequently denied their human rights in both the community and care homes. In addition, people with dementia are not always involved in decision-making processes and their wishes and preferences for care are often not respected.[27] (World Health Organization)

> Dementia does not rob someone of their dignity, it's our reaction to them that does. (Teepa Snow)[28]

DR. ALLEN POWER
GERIATRICIAN, ADVOCATE, AND AUTHOR

Allen Power is an internist and geriatrician. He was recently named Schlegel Chair in Aging and Dementia Innovation at the Schlegel University of Waterloo Research Institute for Aging in Waterloo, Canada. He is an Eden Alternative associate and designed an Eden Alternative course[29] specifically for dementia care that is based on his book entitled *Dementia Beyond Drugs*.[30] Allen also authored *Dementia Beyond Disease*,[31] a book that is based in the Eden Alternative's seven Domains of Well-being. In his books and presentations, Allen shares case studies of successful person-directed care for those living with cognitive challenges that resemble the model we have described at St. John's and those we will cover in the next interview with the Beatitudes Campus leadership. We have chosen to highlight three of the themes that are central to Allen's mission: surplus safety and restraints, non-segregated living for those with dementia, and dedicated staff assignments.

> I define security as supporting both emotional and psychological security. Many restraints have the opposite effect.

Surplus Safety and Restraints

Allen believes that surplus safety leads to the adoption of policies and procedures that are designed through the litigious lens of the worst-case scenario. Safety surplus thinking usually results in the use of physical and/or chemical restraints. Restraints are defined as medication or devices that restrain movement. Some commonly used restraints include antipsychotic medications, alarms, locked doors, bedrails, low chairs that people cannot rise from, and Velcro belts.

According to Allen, approximately 15 percent of Americans who have received the diagnosis of dementia and are living in nursing homes are taking antipsychotic medications, representing approximately 180,000 to 200,000 people. It should be noted that the Centers for Medicare and Medicaid Services include individuals without dementia in their calculations of antipsychotic usage in nursing homes. This dilutes the rate to 15.1 percent. If we looked only at people in nursing homes who have a diagnosis of dementia, the rate would be closer to 25 percent. In his book, *Dementia Beyond Drugs*, Allen writes that, in the US, 4 out of 5 people, or 4,000,000 people, with dementia are living at home or in a retirement community. Based on a study by the US Department of Health and Human Services, 14 percent of that cohort is taking antipsychotics, representing more than 500,000 people. He highlights this number to raise awareness that the overuse of antipsychotic medications is not limited to nursing homes.

The only risk-free environment for humans is a coffin.
(Bill Thomas, Cofounder of the Eden Alternative and the
Green House Project)

Providers must balance quality of life against risk, and they must involve the entire care team, the management, the resident, and the family in the decision because individual priorities will vary. In his interview, Allen gave an example that explains the risk versus quality-of-life balance that Heather Luth, the Dementia Program Coordinator at Schlegel Villages in Canada, experienced.[32] Heather had a resident who was constantly at the door wanting to leave. They tried several person-centered interventions to divert this activity, but none worked. The gentleman was under stress every day. Heather did not want to make a staff-centered solution and drug his stress away, but wanted to meet whatever need he was expressing. He told the staff he wanted to get outside in the fresh air and meet people. Eventually Heather and her team took a big gulp and, with the consent of his family, gave him the key code to the door. Today the resident regularly greets visitors and opens the door for them or just sits outside watching life happen. It is easy to pathologize the needs and desires of a person with cognitive limitations as a behavioral psychotic symptom of dementia. Most, if not all, people would be frustrated being locked inside day and night. Like most people with or without a brain disorder, the resident just wanted to be able to go outside. He has continued this routine for the past four years. In those years, he left the campus and took the bus three times. Fortunately he was safe, and people brought him back. With the new technology of today, if the resident left campus more often, they might consider using a non-invasive GPS tracking device. Allen points out that the trade-off in this situation is the risk of three days of leaving campus versus safety of four years of being stressed by the door and being medicated with dangerous drugs.

We have to understand that, for every person who leaves the home, there are hundreds of people who are being put on antipsychotics who are distressed and traumatized every single day behind a locked door.

In Chap. 6 of *Dementia Beyond Disease*, Allen outlines a seven-step framework that can function as a guide for organizations that are considering unlocking memory care units and desegregating those living with dementia. They include:

1. Hold a discussion of the desired activity and explore its meaning for the person and his/her understanding of the upside and downside risks involved;

2. Explore the person's values and tolerance for risk. Not everyone views risk/reward the same way, so this must be individualized to have any impact;

3. Look for the conditions and resources needed to help empower the person to succeed;

4. Explore a continuum of empowerment, adjusting the parameters to balance autonomy and safety;

5. Make collaborative decisions;

6. Monitor outcomes and adjust the plan as needed;

7. Keep other stakeholders informed of the process.

In his blog series *Hidden Restraint*,[33] Allen describes unlocking doors as a challenge much like the challenges providers faced when they began to untie people from more severe restraints in the 1990s. These changes take a complete operational redesign to remove the structural, relational, and operational factors that contribute to residents wanting to leave. That redesign is neither quick nor easy, but it is possible. At its best, it will include a home-like setting and a care culture that fulfills the Eden Alternative's seven Domains of Well-being, including identity, connectedness, security, autonomy, meaning, growth, and joy. In blog three, Allen gives two compelling case studies of providers who chose to unlock the doors of their memory care areas.[34] We urge you to read them for inspiration.

Antipsychotics can double the risk of death and triple the risk of stroke in people with dementia, heavily sedate them, and accelerate cognitive decline. (Jeremy Wright, Chairman of the All-Party Parliamentary Group on Dementia, United Kingdom[35])

Restraints do not provide security and peace of mind to the resident who is being restrained. The sobering irony of chemical and physical restraints is that they have been proven to not increase safety and, in many cases, to put the person at greater risk.[36,37,38,39] According to Allen, restraints have proven to increase the risk of serious injuries, emotional distress, bedsores, incontinence, and muscle wasting. The research findings about restraints led government insurers and providers to reduce the use of physical restraints and antipsychotic medications. Hopefully this trend will continue as more and more providers seek person-centered, less invasive interventions to meet the needs of their clients.

In many ways, we are reinforcing the stigmas and fears by locking up people whose brains have changed. People with dementia deserve to be seen for who they are beyond their limitations.

Philosophy of Segregation

Allen does not think that people with dementia should be segregated from society and their communities, including care communities. He believes that segregating people reinforces the negative stereotypes of dementia held by clinicians and the public that those with cognitive challenges are no longer equal. Allen addresses this issue often in his publications and speaking engagements. He feels strongly that it is an issue of human rights and is confident in his beliefs because he has seen many examples of providers who do not segregate and by doing so have greatly improved the well-being of the residents.

> The best providers to those living with dementia understand that it is about preserving people's humanity as much as possible.

Dedicated Staff Assignments

Another factor that contributes to well-being is connected relationships that are formed when staff does not rotate. Maintaining a dedicated staff assignment is a vital component of person-centered care. It is a reoccurring theme in this chapter because it is so important. A dedicated staff is one that does not rotate; care partners work with the same individuals each day. A resident does not have the invasive experience of having new unknown individuals helping them with private and intimate activities.

When a person living in a long-term care residence exhibits combative or aggressive behavior, the care team knows the person well enough to understand that they are in pain, are hungry, or are agitated. The care team is also so acutely familiar with the daily habits,

tendencies, and preferences of the residents that they can often anticipate needs and meet those needs before the resident becomes agitated.
Because they are with the same residents every day, care partners
might know whether a resident likes to sleep in late, would like ice
cream, wants to sing, move around, or to smoke a cigarette. If the care
partner needs to take the person to a balcony or out to the courtyard
to smoke, they will do so. In our interview, Allen shared the story of
Arcare's transition to dedicated staff assignments and the surprising
outcomes they realized as a result.

It takes a community—a relationship-centered approach to
celebrating and supporting old age. (Daniella Greenwood)

Daniella Greenwood is the Dementia Strategy and Innovation
Manager at Arcare Aged Care in Australia.[40] Arcare has 27 residential care communities in Victoria and Queensland. From 2012
to 2013, Arcare surveyed their staff and their residents and family members to determine what components of care were the most
important to them. The research shows four categories of importance. One was identified as connections. Many comments that were
written mentioned the importance of continuous relationships. The
survey findings about the importance of connected relationships led
Arcare to transform their culture by implementing a dedicated staff
assignment model throughout their organization. Three aspects of
the model are:

• Employees work a minimum of three shifts per week;
• Every employee, including the care team and the catering team,

works with exactly the same small group of residents every time they come to work;

- Residents and their families are continually encouraged to provide feedback to their care team.

Much to their delight, not only did the culture change increase staff, family, and resident satisfaction, it yielded commanding health and financial benefits. The transformation had early promising results; one community of 38 residents found that within only six weeks, the staff was able to spend more time with the elders without sacrificing their task completion.

Outcomes for staff included:

- 19.8 percent increase in job satisfaction for the care team, not including nurses;
- 30 percent increase in job satisfaction for the nurses.

Financial outcomes by reducing operating cost included:

- 50.2 percent reduction in staff turnover;
- 27.5 percent reduction in sick leave;
- Average decrease in day and evening care partners of 28 per month. (In one area the staff needed decreased by 46 percent, from 48 to 26.)

Family satisfaction outcomes were:

- 45 percent increase in family satisfaction;
- 100 percent decrease in formal complaints by family members.

The health outcomes for residents of one early adopting community included:

- 69 percent decrease in chest infections;
- 90 percent decrease in pressure sores;
- 25 percent reduction in skin tears;
- 12.9 percent reduction in falls;
- 6 pound average weight gain;
- 51.6 percent reduction in psychotropic medication use.

Arcare continually audits their communities to ensure that they are promoting meaningful connections for their staff, the elders, and the families. They have been recognized for the level of care they provide, and Daniella is a sought-after lecturer throughout the world.

Housekeepers often remain an untapped source of care and safety. (Tena Alonzo, Beatitudes Campus)

Another glowing example of a provider that uses a dedicated staff is Beatitudes Campus. All of the staff from grounds people to physicians are trained in person-centered care. One story that registered nurse Karen Mitchell tells that spotlights the importance of the training is about a housekeeper. One day when Karen was working as a nurse, the housekeeper asked her to check on a patient. Karen conducted a basic assessment but did not find anything of concern. She pressed the housekeeper to tell her what was worrying her. The response was, Mrs. M is not singing this morning. She sings every morning. Because of this feedback Karen kept a close eye on Mrs. M who developed a temperature the next day due to a urinary tract infection. The housekeeper knew the resident and her habits so well that she was able to recognize the early signs of discomfort.

TENA M. ALONZO, KAREN MITCHELL, AND IVAN HILTON BEATITUDES CAMPUS

Tena Alonzo is the Director of Education and Research and the Director of the Comfort Matters™ program at Beatitudes Campus.[41] Karen Mitchell is an Educator of Comfort Matters.[42] Ivan Hilton is the Director of Business Development for Comfort Matters.

The Phoenix, Arizona-based Beatitudes Campus is a life plan community (sometimes referred to as a continuing care retirement community) with 700 residents. The long-term care residences of Beatitudes Campus are brilliant examples of fully person-centered care and have similar characteristics and outcomes to those that we have outlined earlier in this chapter. We wish to highlight two specific areas of excellence of the care team at Beatitudes Campus; the elimination of sundowning in their memory care and their Comfort Matters research and training.

Sundowning

Sundowning or sundowning syndrome is the tendency for someone living with dementia to become agitated, confused, or hyperactive in the late afternoon or early evening. Some attribute this behavior to the sleep disturbances that are often experienced with those living with dementia. Some people, like Allen Power and the staff of Beatitudes Campus, are convinced that sundowning is caused by a care culture imposed by the provider that is not in sync with the changing rhythms and cognition of residents with dementia. Beatitudes Campus has eliminated all cases of sundowning in their memory care communities. They have done this by employing a high degree of person-centered care.

People living with dementia do not have the same tolerance for boredom and agitation. We are mindful of tolerance.
(Karen Mitchell)

Many people with dementia do not have the capacity to rationalize their way out of bad moods or to delay gratification. If a resident who likes to sleep late has the housecleaning staff banging around while cleaning the room early in the morning, that resident would become grumpy. They also may become tired and agitated in the late afternoon or early evening. This would be the case for any other person, with or without dementia, who is not a morning person. If a resident of Beatitudes Campus memory care is not a morning person, no one wakes that resident until the resident wants to rise. The staff knows the rhythms of each resident and adapts to those rhythms, rather than making a person with cognitive difficulties adapt to the preferences or convenience of the care team. This places the well-being of the resident in the center of the care plan and execution. There is no shower or other schedule imposed on the residents by the Beatitudes care team. It takes a fluid and adaptive care team that does not rotate to individualize the day according to rhythms and preferences of each resident.

When frail people are on many medications, it can make them feel ill and not want to eat. Without a healthy amount of nutrition, a person could become agitated in the latter part of the day. Residents in the memory care communities at Beatitudes Campus take far fewer medications than the national average. This contributes to a healthier appetite and weight gain. Another contributing factor to mitigate wasting is liberalized diets. The care team of Beatitudes Campus encourages residents to eat whatever and whenever they like. If a resident wants to eat a chocolate bar at midnight, they are given a chocolate bar. The care team prepares meals around the clock in the kitchen located in the residence.

On my visit, I noticed an easily accessible ice cream freezer that was stocked with a variety of ice cream bars and sandwiches. Another freezer held a selection of cookie dough. Whenever a resident wants to bake and eat warm cookies, they do so with a care partner. When a person is allowed to eat when they feel like eating and what they want to eat, they are less likely to become agitated and experience sundowning.

> When a person feels sick or tired most of the time, they are prone to sundowning. (Tena Alonzo)

Antipsychotic medications slow a person down, which accounts for some of the sundowning that is pervasive in many long-term care homes globally. Like the person-centered care models we have already profiled, Beatitudes Campus uses little or no antipsychotic, anxiolytic, or sedative medications. Some residents arrive already taking such medications, which accounts for the fact Beatitudes Campus cannot claim zero percent usage at all times. Eventually the new residents acclimate to the care culture and have no need of those types of medications.

Another crucial aspect of person-centered care is identifying pain. Often people who are living with dementia are not able to communicate that they are in pain. Their communication can come in many forms, including agitation, confusion, and moving around. If these behaviors occur in the late afternoon or early evening, they are labeled as sundowning. The Beatitudes Campus program, Comfort Matters, was designed as a palliative care model for organizations that provide care for those living with dementia. The care setting can be in any location. A featured component of Comfort Matters is training the care team to identify pain. A staff that does not rotate and that is trained in pain identification will likely know a patient well enough that they can spot any sign of pain and administer Tylenol before the agitation and sun-downing begins.

Comfort Matters

In 2005, the management and care team of Beatitudes Campus began to research and transform the way they cared for and interacted with individuals with dementia who live in their 700-person campus and in a private home. Beatitudes has two residences that are dedicated solely to those with dementia. The average age of the other approximately 660 independent living residents is 85. Tena and Karen estimate that approximately 65 percent of that population has some stage of memory issues. Their research led them to build an organizational care model based in comfort and well-being named Comfort Matters. The purpose of palliative care is to provide support and comfort by relieving pain and the stresses of illness for someone living with a long-term or chronic condition. In 2012, the Alzheimer's Association New York City Chapter (now named CaringKind) collaborated with Beatitudes Campus to study palliative care through the lens of dementia. Eventually they began a project, which is still in process, that consists of the Beatitudes Campus team providing 30 months of training and staff coaching, while the Comfort Matters model is implemented in three New York area nursing homes.[43] The implementation is being measured for many health and satisfaction outcomes. The results to date are promising. In 2010, LeadingAge honored Comfort Matters with the Excellence in Research and Education award. In 2013, LeadingAge honored Comfort Matters with the Public Trust Award.

Tena and Karen, along with the Comfort Matters team, built an interdisciplinary evidence-based educational program to help caregivers and care providers implement Comfort Matters. The Comfort Matters training team coaches providers for the period of two years as they navigate through the course material and undertake organizational culture change. In 2016, the Horizon House in Seattle, Washington, became the first Comfort Matters Accredited Organization.[44] In the past 16 months, 12 care providers have begun their journey of implementation and accreditation by Comfort Matters. Tena and Karen and the Comfort Matters team have hosted numerous delegations of long-term care providers from Europe and Asia. It is our hope that Comfort Matters will become the standard of care for all people living with dementia.

Barriers to Person-Centered Care

Culture change in an established organization or health system is always a challenge. To become person-centered, the institutional process must be broken down to a fluid relationship between management and the care team. Processes have to be flexible to meet the individual needs of each resident.

Culture change must be adopted throughout an entire organization with buy-in from senior management and the board. This process is lengthy, and without continual reinforcement may not be successful because it can be tempting to slide back to the old ways of doing things.

A not so obvious challenge lies in combating the stigma of dementia and of older individuals that can act as a cultural plague. When the care team treats the residents with parental control that is based around the belief that cognitive challenges or frailty make a person less whole, rather than respecting them for who they are and honoring the lives they have led, the care will not be person-centered. Their policies and procedures will not be built around the well-being of the residents.

On first thought, providers might think that adopting a new culture would be more costly. As demonstrated by Signature Health, St. John's, Arcare, Beatitudes Campus, the Green House Project, and other providers that we did not include in this chapter, person-centered long-term care presents the opportunity to have better outcomes at a lower price and the need for fewer care staff. It is our hope that these examples will inspire a greater adoption of person-centered long-term care and eventually become an expected standard of care both in the US and internationally.

Providing access to palliative care and bringing care to the home that enables older adults to age in place, direct their own care plan, and experience their final days in the place of their own choosing is one of the highest forms of person-centered care. In the next chapter, we write about the growth and gap of palliative care around the world and describe models of home-based care that improve access and increase well-being while substantially reducing care costs.

The full interviews referenced in this chapter can be found at this link: www.accessh.org/agingwell.

5

Home-Based Palliative Care and Aging in Place and Community

Palliative Care

Palliative care provides health care and emotional support to those living with a serious illness and their families throughout the course of the illness and often the patient's life. Palliative care is a form of patient-centered long-term care that prioritizes the quality of life of the patient. It is not limited to older adults, but for the purpose of this book, we will focus on palliative care for those 65 and older. Palliative care is designed to treat the whole person, not just their medical concerns. It combines coordinated care management with psychological support for patients and their families as they navigate life with serious illness. Psychological support includes help with stress or depression. Both are critical quality-of-life concerns that are often overlooked in traditional care. Other features of a good palliative care program include around-the-clock access to a clinician, care that is coordinated across multiple specialties, and care that is aligned with the priorities of the patient—including end-of-life preferences.

> The good physician treats the disease; the great physician treats the patient who has the disease. (William Osler, Founding Professor, Johns Hopkins Hospital)

Palliative care is a vital component of a well-functioning healthcare system, but access to palliative care is scant throughout the world. Part of the reason for this care gap is the increase in life expectancy. There was an approximate 30-year gain in life expectancy between 1900 and 2000. This seems like a long time to realize such a gain, but it is almost equal to the gain attained over the preceding 5,000 years.[1] The relatively rapid change has left health systems unable to meet the complex care needs for older adults living with multiple chronic illnesses. The care gap can also be attributed to the fact that people used to die from many diseases that they now are able to live with for decades. Additionally, some of these diseases are increasing in occurrence due to alcohol abuse, smoking, and obesity. The ability to live with many diseases is a brilliant feat of modern health care, but it is beneficial only if there is quality of life in the added years. This represents the difference between lifespan and healthspan.

> The goal of palliative care is to help people living with serious illness to have the best possible quality of life: in other words, to live as well as possible for as long as possible. (Diane E. Meier)

Estimates claim that in the high-income countries, 69 to 82 percent of people who die would benefit from palliative care.[2] Some claim that if everyone had access to palliative care as we understand it today, the lives of 100 million people would be improved.[3] In 2014, the World Health Assembly established the first global resolution on palliative care. The resolution calls for the World Health Organization and member states to integrate palliative care as a central element of their health systems with a focus on primary care systems and healthcare delivery in the community and home.[4]

It is imperative that institutions update their medical education and training to prepare students to meet the need for palliative care in all settings. It is long overdue for health providers to adapt to the demographic shift by building lower-cost systems of accessible, coordinated care that can serve the older population with high rates of comorbidity. These systems must have the capacity to honor the late life care plan and priorities of each individual. To accomplish palliative care penetration on the scale needed, we must adjust our collective vision from a medicalized cure mentality to one of care and support.

> We are increasingly moving away from fee-for-service because of the recognition that it is bankrupting our society and it is not meeting the healthcare needs of patients and families. (Diane E. Meier)

Cost Outcomes of Palliative Care

Five percent of the most ill patients living with multiple chronic conditions and functional limitations account for 60 percent of the total cost of health care in the United States.[5] Eighty-nine percent of this population will live for more than a year.[6] Palliative care not only enables a better quality of life for people living with illness and their families, but it is value-based care that can substantially lower healthcare costs. This savings is most effective when care is delivered in the home setting. It is possible to take care of three people in their home for the same cost as keeping one person in a long-term care residence.[7] When care is coordinated across the continuum, it is more efficient and reduces redundancies, medical error, unnecessary care, length of hospital stays, hospitalizations, emergency department visits, overall healthcare utilization, patient depression and pain, and conflicting care and medications.[8,9]

Overtreatment and overtesting raise healthcare costs for insurers and also for the patients and their families. In the US, overtreatment results in each household paying thousands of dollars out of pocket for unnecessary care each year.[10] Not all families can bear the brunt of the costs without compromising on other important spending such as food, education, and their own health care. This drives an increase in the social determinants that lead to poor health, which eventually costs the healthcare system more in the long run. It should be noted that out-of-pocket costs impact lower-income households more strongly than medium- and upper-income households, thus perpetuating a cycle of poverty.

> Hospitals should be the place of last resort, not the only resort. (Diane E. Meier)

Emergency department visits, hospital readmissions, and care transitions are reoccurring themes in this and other chapters because all markedly increase the cost of care and do not necessarily contribute to better health or quality of life for older patients. Palliative care provides patients with access to medical support around the clock. The access to care clinicians after hours gives patients better options than an ambulance transport and emergency department visit for a health crisis that could have been avoided with coordinated accessible care or could have been treated at home by a caregiver, family member, or the palliative care team. Palliative care teams are trained to anticipate predictable health complications and prepare for them in advance by monitoring specific symptoms and health measures. Dr. Kristofer Smith and his team at Northwell Health also stock medications and medical equipment in the home in preparation for predictable adverse health events that can be handled by a family member or caregiver. This helps patients avoid the cycle of emergency department visit, subsequent hospitalization, care transition to skilled nursing, and care transition to the home.

Medical errors are the third leading cause of death in the US.[11] Hospitals and emergency departments are dangerous and expensive environments for older frail people who are cognitively and immunologically vulnerable. These settings can cause infection, confusion, delirium, and falls, which increase the care costs and care need. The accompanying health decline can often lead to the patient transitioning to expensive skilled nursing care before they make it back home, if they do make it home. This cycle causes suffering and is remarkably expensive.

As we mentioned in Chap. 1, 80 percent of people prefer to die at home, while few do. This is because there are not systems in place to honor the desire to age in place and die at home. Dying in a clinical setting is also far more expensive. People who die in the hospital incur costs that are 7 times that of those who die at home.[12] Throughout the end-of-life process, many people receive overtreatment and unnecessary and even harmful care. End-of-life care planning and systems that support the wishes of the patient and the family can help people avoid unwanted, invasive care and generate substantial cost savings.

The 1997 seminal report by the Institute of Medicine (IOM),

Approaching Death: Improving Care at the End of Life,[13] shined a ground-breaking spotlight on the suffering caused by too much costly care at the end of life that neither improves quality of life nor extends the length of life. Since its publication, and the 2014 publication by the IOM, *Dying in America: Improving Quality and Honoring Individual Preferences Near the End of Life*,[14] awareness has increased and palliative care has become more available for all life stages, but the response still falls exceedingly short of the need.

Patient Engagement and End-of-Life Care

Palliative care falls under the umbrella of person-centered care because it is based in individualized coordinated care that is designed to meet and adapt to the changing priorities of the patient. This includes advanced care planning that involves soliciting, understanding, and honoring how and where the patient wishes to live out the last months of life. Advanced care planning is an invaluable element that helps to meet the goal of well-being for older people living with advanced illness. Honoring the end-of-life preferences of the patient is important from a human standpoint and is also financially impactful.

Atul Gawande, MD, MPH,[15] advocates for care systems that are designed to honor the priorities of the patients throughout the end of life. He is the author of four *New York Times* best sellers, including *Being Mortal: Medicine and What Matters in the End*. In his testimony before the US Senate Special Committee on Aging for the hearing entitled "The Right Care at the Right Time: Ensuring Person-Centered Care for Individuals with Serious Illness,"[16] Gawande stressed the need for physicians to have discussions with their patients about their care priorities. He noted that these important fact-gathering conversations occur less than one third of the time before a person's death, resulting in care that does not align with what is most important to the patient.

Gawande also noted that when care aligns with a patient's priorities, people feel more in control, they experience less anxiety and depression, and they spend more time at home and with family. Additionally, patients often live longer.[17] Usually, when asked, many people will opt out of invasive procedures and medications that are not life-saving and often do not prolong a life of any quality. Procedures that focus more on disease control than quality of life do not even help people live longer. They cause more suffering; patients experience more pain, more anxiety, more unnecessary care, and more hospitalizations.[18]

Despite this knowledge and efforts by insurers and health systems to meet the need of palliative care for the increasing older population, a considerable care gap still exists today. This gap is most prominent in the community setting, which is any setting that is not the hospital, including office practices, cancer centers, dialysis centers, nursing homes, assisted living facilities, and care in the home.

Hospitals with palliative care programs have resulted in shorter lengths of stays, fewer intensive care admissions, and lower laboratory and pharmacy costs.[19] On a more hopeful note, due in large part to the efforts of Dr. Diane E. Meier and the Center to Advance Palliative Care, the number of hospital-based palliative care programs in the US has more than tripled in the past decade. Today, in the US, 70 percent of hospitals with more than 50 beds have a palliative care team. This is a promising advancement that we hope will continue to expand and progress in hospitals nationally and around the world.

The Center to Advance Palliative Care is leaping into the quality chasm facing those living with serious illness, and trying to close it. (Diane E. Meier)

DR. DIANE E. MEIER
THE CENTER TO ADVANCE PALLIATIVE CARE

Diane E. Meier is the Director of the Center to Advance Palliative Care (CAPC).[20] She is also Vice Chair for Public Policy, Professor of Geriatrics and Palliative Medicine, and the Catherine Gaisman Professor of Medical Ethics at the Icahn School of Medicine at Mount Sinai in New York City.

The CAPC is an international non-profit organization within the Icahn School of Medicine at Mount Sinai. The Center fosters the awareness and integration of palliative care programs in all care settings. CAPC serves as a resource for education, training, tools, and technical assistance. It is an organization with 900 healthcare provider members. CAPC has designated 11 Palliative Care Leadership Centers around the country that educate and train organizations planning to develop sustainable palliative care programs. The Center also houses a directory of palliative care providers in the US. CAPC acts as a think tank and a convener of thought leaders to distill best practices into transferrable skill sets and share the information. Diane refers to this practice as the facilitation or diffusion of innovation.

We have a healthcare system that was designed 65 years ago around curable, fixable, and surgical problems. It fails to address the whole person care needs of the tens of millions of people with serious and often multiple chronic illnesses who are living a long time.

Patient Priorities

A palliative care team has an ongoing conversation with their patients to understand their changing life priorities. These priorities are weighed against the outcomes of procedures and the side effects of medications. This is a variation on the theme of risk surplus that we described in the Allen Power section of Chap. 1. It also echoes the patient-centered long-term care philosophies from the same chapter. Diane explains the situation that she faces with her patients:

> When I ask patients and families what is most important, I will hear answers such as, "I want to leave the hospital and go home to my garden." Patients also say, "I want to see my youngest grandson graduate from college" or "I want to connect with my brother whom I have not spoken to in 30 years." I have never had someone say to me, "I want to live forever." Yet, the entire healthcare system is designed as if everyone wants to live for-ever. The factors that matter most to patients and families are completely ignored because we don't ask. How could we possibly design a person-centered care plan without the key concerns of the patient in the forefront?

Palliative care in the form of hospice is care and support in the last six months of life. Although it is widely available, due to poor patient management and regulations, 30 percent of those who receive hospice in the US receive it for only one week. The national median length of hospice stay is only 17.4 days.[21] Another barrier to patients transition-ing to hospice care is the Medicare requirement that two doctors state the patient is likely to die in a short time. These predictions are not easy or reliable so physicians often do not make them. Without the support of hospice, patients often fall victim to the cycle of home, emergency department, hospitalization, and skilled nursing throughout their last couple of months of life.

Diane shared a *New York Times* article that documented this far too common cycle caused by the inability of the healthcare system, as it is structured today, to honor people's preferences. In the article, "Fighting to Honor a Father's Last Wish: To Die at Home,"[22] author Nina Bernstein recounts the heartbreaking and unsuccessful efforts by a daughter to honor her father's care plan in the last two years of his life. The article is a perfect example of what most seniors experience in the last two years of life. The comments by the readers expressed outrage. Many people who commented had similar life experiences themselves. It is Diane's belief that people, as healthcare customers and stakeholders, will become a driving force in the expansion of more accessible palliative and late-life care.

Education and Training

Physicians and other members of the palliative care team are trained to offer emotional support to their patients and their families. They are skilled in symptom management, including fatigue, depression, and difficulty sleeping. Family members, who are often seniors themselves, also experience these symptoms. They feel overwhelmed with the task of managing a serious illness. They might have had to leave the workforce. They are living with the fear of losing their family member. They are likely facing the financial ramifications of out-of-pocket costs and lost employment.

Diane reminds us of the daunting education gap within the professional community. She asserts that palliative care training and education should be a prominent part of every medical school, nursing program, and all other clinical care education programs. When medical education is solely focused on curing an illness, symptom management is not given enough educational and training attention. Doctors and nurses need symptom management expertise because many symptoms of chronic illness such as pain, nausea, exhaustion, depression, stress, and others will last throughout the lifetime of a patient. Additionally, all clinicians need to be trained in how to have the conversations to learn what is most important to the patient and family, and how to navigate and document these discussions to build a patient-centered care plan.

Hofstra-Northwell School of Medicine[23] is an example of a medical school that designed a curriculum to prepare physicians to thrive in the new era of medicine with a focus on aging care and community-based delivery. Other medical schools are using the CAPC education programs in a flipped classroom style where the students study online and use classroom time to practice palliative care skills and review case studies.

Palliative Care at Home

Diane explained that most home care is provided by home health agencies that are not delivering primary or palliative care. CAPC and other palliative care advocates are encouraging payers, including Medicare and Medicaid, to reimburse for palliative care in the home. Dr. Kristofer Smith has been making house calls for 15 years. His commitment to delivering the right care at the right time and in the right setting continues today at Northwell Health Solutions.

Health care is finally understanding that the house call is not a nostalgic nod to the past but rather an essential care model for those who are most vulnerable. (Dr. Kristofer Smith)

DR. KRISTOFER SMITH
NORTHWELL HEALTH SOLUTIONS

Dr. Kristofer Smith is the Senior Vice President of the Office of Population Clinical-Health Management and the Medical Director for Northwell Health Solutions, the largest integrated health delivery system in New York State.

He is also an Associate Professor in the Department of Medicine at the Hofstra-Northwell School of Medicine. The CAPC designated Northwell Health Solutions a Palliative Care Learning Center. This offers Kristofer and his team a structured way in which to teach their palliative care models to organizations around the world.

As part of their commitment toward value-based care that meets the triple aim of lower cost, better outcomes (including patient satisfaction), and increased access, the Centers for Medicare and Medicaid Innovation (CMMI) funded a 15-site demonstration project named Independence at Home.[24] The goal of the demonstration is to determine whether a primary care program can yield value-based outcomes for Medicare patients with multiple chronic conditions and cognitive and functional impairments. The program is considered home-based palliative care because primary care and palliative care are one in the same for this patient population. Nine of the 17 participating sites realized more than US$25 million in savings in the first year of the demonstration.[25] In year two, the demonstration served more than 10,000 patients and saved Medicare more than US$10 million, representing an average US$1,010 per beneficiary. Seven of the participating practices will share in incentive payments totaling US$5.7 million. Centers for Medicare and Medicaid Services (CMS) also measured the quality outcomes of each demonstration site. All of the providers showed quality improvements in at least two measures, while four practices showed improvement in all measures.[26]

The measures include:

- Provider makes contact with the patient within 48 hours of hospital admission, hospital discharge, or emergency department visit;
- Patient has fewer hospital readmissions within 30 days;
- Provider identifies a patient's medication within 48 hours of hospital discharge;
- Provider documents the preferences of the patient;
- Provider uses inpatient hospital and emergency departments less often when treating conditions such as diabetes, high blood pressure, asthma, pneumonia, and urinary tract infection.

Northwell Health Solutions serves approximately 1,400 patients each year in their home-based primary care division.[27] A subset of approximately 350 to 400 of those patients participate in the Independence at Home demonstration. The mission of the home-based primary care program is to:

- Provide patient and family-centered care;
- Maintain or improve functional capacity;
- Reduce unwanted and unnecessary care;
- Increase the days a patient spends in their home;
- Facilitate death with dignity at home.

My job is to understand how to make all the programs in between hospice and regular ambulatory care self-sustaining financially.

POPULATION HEALTH

Kristofer Smith and his team identify the frailest patients who need a better healthcare option. This population is often cycling from home to hospital to skilled nursing and back home. They are receiving care in the least optimal settings while realizing poor outcomes and poor quality of life. Kristofer and his team bring these individuals a higher intensity person-centered care model that is tailored to the priorities of the patients and their families. The care plan is dynamically aligned with the patient's changing health status. This program fills the two-year, on average, care gap between ambulatory and hospice care (Fig. 5.1). Home-based primary care would not be financially sustainable under a fee-for-service reimbursement model. It has only been made possible in recent years since the passage of legislation in support of value-based care and the resulting alternate payment models. This reimbursement evolution presents better opportunities for providers to meet the care and support needs of their older population.

The average age of the patients in the home-based primary care program is 86. Sixty-three percent need assistance with five to six activities of daily living.[28] They have a median survival rate of two years, which means they do not yet qualify for hospice. They are two thirds female. They are living with illnesses that are so advanced that it is difficult for them to leave their homes and travel to ambulatory practices.

Fig. 5.1. Palliative care gap

Our patients are usually older, frail, and have multiple chronic conditions. We titrate the intensity of the care model for patients.

Challenges to Home-Based Palliative Care

One of the challenges of the home-based primary care program is making sure that patients are in the right program. If a lower-cost patient is placed in a higher-cost program, the opportunity for cost savings is lost. The home-based primary care program of Northwell Health Solutions costs US$4,000 per patient per year. If a high-cost patient enters that program, the opportunity for cost savings is substantial and can make the program self-sustaining.

Another challenge that home-based primary care presents is

convincing the patients and their families to call the care team when they experience a health crisis. Patients and families are accustomed to dialing 911 when they are in distress. They have not had any other option for their whole lives. Kristofer discussed the need for the care team to build trust with the patients and their families. The around-the-clock availability decreases emergency department visits and readmissions and keeps their patients out of the cycle of dangerous care and in their homes instead. The program is fundamentally about the reduction of suffering.

The providers of the home-based primary care coordinate all of the care of the patient to avoid care fragmentation. The program uses a team consisting of medical coordinators, physicians, nurses, social workers, and nurse practitioners. The physicians make 110 house call visits per month. The frequency of the other team members depends on the care needs of the patients. This type of home-based primary care would be difficult for a smaller provider organization to offer because of the need for a highly trained care team and the administrative infrastructure to measure outcomes and monitor the changing health profiles of the patients.

Pending Legislation and New Payment Models

Kristofer and his team at Northwell Health Solutions and the other successful Independence at Home providers have been so successful in delivering higher-quality care outcomes at a lower cost that, in July of 2016, a bipartisan group of senators[29] introduced legislation[30] to make Independence at Home a permanent benefit within the Medicare program. Additionally, Kristofer, as part of the model design team with the Coalition to Transform Advanced Care (CTAC), recently received support from Medicare's Physician-Focused Payment Model Technical Advisory Committee to implement a community and home-based palliative care model for Medicare fee-for-service patients. It is our hope that this happens and that community-based palliative care becomes the normal standard of care.

Aging in Place and Community

Home-based palliative and primary care enables aging in place. Approximately 90 percent of older adults want to stay at home throughout the course of their lives.[31] Aging in community is a concept based in the understanding that simply being able to stay in one's home is not enough, and that people need personal and societal connections. For the past 30 years, Dr. Allan Teel has been facilitating aging in place with a strong community connection component.

DR. ALLAN TEEL
FULL CIRCLE AMERICA

Dr. Allan Teel is the founder of Full Circle America and the author of *Alone and Invisible No More*. As a home healthcare visionary, he has been enabling his older, frail patients to receive palliative care and support in their homes for the past 30 years. His high-tech, high-touch approach makes use of advanced technology and preexisting community supports and services to build a comprehensive circle of care and social support. The care plan is managed in partnership with the client's existing clinical team.

Technology

Allan uses the business-to-business facing Bliss CONNECT technology[32] to coordinate care and community support for his clients. After his Sloan MIT fellowship, Pankaj Khare spent seven years designing a coordinated care platform that enables health care at home, aging in place and community, long-term care, and disability support. The platform is fully customizable and is device agnostic. The Full Circle America Bliss CONNECT mission is to operationalize an affordable support solution with an eye on population health while paying attention to some of the healthcare metrics they designed. Their main focus is putting older adults and their families at the center of the healthcare ecosystem.

The technology can be loaded onto a basic user-friendly tablet. The platform home page is much like a social networking site. Users are able to chat and share photos in a Facebook-style communication board, send and receive emails, and connect to any outside internet sites. The user can add an endless array of apps, customized to their preferences, to the home page for convenience.

With a finger tap, the user is able to videoconference, teleconference, and e-chat with their care team. The care team includes a doctor, a nurse, a case manager, and all others involved in the older adult's care, including family, neighbors, and volunteers. The complete medical, health, insurance, and billing records are stored in real time on the platform. The program also has panic call and medicine reminder options.

Passive and active video monitoring devices along with motion sensors can be connected through the tablet and sent directly to the care team to be stored on the platform.

Early on, it became crystal clear to me that neighbors and friends had to be a big part of the solution.

Community Assets

One aspect that makes Full Circle America successful and better than some homecare providers is that Allan addresses not just the physical needs of his patients, but he cares for the whole person and finds ways to support their psychological, social, and environmental needs by connecting his patients to their own community assets. Allan believes strongly in the importance of combining health care and social supports under one roof. If the patient needs home modifications to be able to remain at home and move about the house, he will recommend such installations. Allan mentioned that it is important to involve the community to divide the health and social needs of his patients into smaller pieces because families are often not able to take on all of the additional responsibility. In approximately an hour or two of research, Allan maps the existing supportive social services that are available locally for each of his patients. He begins by looking for volunteers within the social circle of the patient, including friends, family members, neighbors, and fellow church members. His next step is to move out into the community to locate volunteer opportunities that fulfill his patients' need for purpose and generativity.[33] Some patients wish to volunteer in schools, police departments, fire departments, and senior centers. Some volunteer to visit Allan's other patients via telephone or in person, creating strong peer-to-peer support relationships. Allan then locates other local supports, including YMCAs, churches, libraries, and schools. These organizations have age-friendly programming and create intergenerational community connections. They are an inexpensive and effective method of addressing loneliness. All of the community connections are housed and accessible on the Bliss CONNECT platform of the patient.

Outcomes

The outcomes of the Full Circle America model include better access to care, patient satisfaction, and improved quality of life. His model reduces emergency department visits and hospital readmissions. The Full Circle America services average US$3,600 to US$9,600 per year depending on the need. This gives his patients a far less expensive option than moving into assisted living and long-term care communities. Allan occasionally refers to his services as virtual assisted living.

Barriers to Uptake and Implementation of Home-Based Palliative Care

Lack of knowledge by the public and healthcare professionals represent a powerful barrier to the use and implementation of palliative care. Seventy percent of Americans reported that they are "not knowledgeable" about palliative care and most healthcare workers think that palliative care and end-of-life care are the same.[34] Another barrier is that there are not enough healthcare professionals who are trained and educated in palliative care.

For palliative care to be accessible in all care settings, it requires a health system redesign and a more holistic view of elder care. Culture change is an ongoing challenge and barrier within healthcare transformation. Possibly the change will be driven by the stakeholders, but it must be supported by reimbursement policy so that health providers are able to implement programs that are sustainable.

Reimbursement policy remains a barrier in access to palliative care for many. The Medicare long-term benefit structure is geared to push patients who are nearing end of life into hospitalization or skilled nursing rather than hospice care, because Medicare will not reimburse the cost of nursing home or assisted living housing expenses. It reimburses only for the hospice care provided. Often people nearing the end of life cannot move home alone or with an older spouse while receiving the only periodic hospice care that is reimbursed. Medicaid will reimburse for housing for those they insure who have depleted their savings, but the process for obtaining this insurance is long and complicated and is often not in place soon enough for the patient.

The shift from fee-for-service to value-based care has opened up many more possibilities for people to remain at home through the end of life, but this is just the beginning of meeting the need. In the six or seven years that the Centers for Medicare and Medicaid Innovation have been conducting demonstrations, none of the models have led to a reimbursement change. The political leadership of the US can profoundly affect the advancement of palliative care access. Many palliative care providers are nervous about what may happen as the Affordable Care Act hangs in the balance. The House and Senate leadership must not allow themselves to be swayed by lobbying entities that will lose money under newer and better models of palliative care. We hope that this chapter inspires health systems to rise to the call of the motto of the CAPC: "Palliative Care Everywhere."

Another way to improve access to care and health outcomes while lowering healthcare spending is coordinated, person-centered, technology-enabled primary care. In the next chapter, we describe the patient-centered medical home and how providers can become accredited by the National Committee for Quality Assurance. We also write about the Veterans Administration's commitment to ensuring that the nation's veterans receive care when and where they need it.

The full interviews referenced in this chapter can be found at this link: www.accessh.org/agingwell.

6

Coordinated Primary Care

Health systems nationally and globally are experiencing the need for higher performing, fully integrated primary care practices. Two main drivers of the need are the growing older population using more care and the shortage in the healthcare workforce, including physicians.[1] In 2014, the United States had a shortage of 8,073 primary care physicians.[2] Some project that by 2025, the US will need 14,900 to 52,000 more primary care physicians.[3,4,5] Coordinated primary care is advantageous for everyone, but especially so for older patients with comorbidities and functional and cognitive limitations. Between 2000 and 2002, the average Medicare beneficiary saw two primary care physicians and five specialists annually.[6] They also accessed other health services, including diagnostics and pharmacy. Older adults are often unable to navigate a fragmented continuum of health care that includes multiple clinicians and medications. They need a single primary care office to provide coordination across specialties and care settings. Coordinated care optimizes health outcomes and has been shown to reduce health expenditures and unnecessary and redundant healthcare utilization.

This chapter overlaps with our chapter on palliative care because, as previously noted, palliative care and primary care for the older population with chronic conditions are one and the same. Other recurring themes in this chapter are value-based and person-centered care and the financial incentives for such care. Coordinated, efficient primary care is inherently value-based and person-centered. The focus of this chapter is on health system organization and quality measures that support coordinated primary care. Patient-centered medical homes are leading the transformation to coordinated healthcare delivery in the US and abroad. Medical homes can enable primary care practices to achieve the triple aim of lower costs, better health outcomes (including patient satisfaction), and increased access to care.[7]

> The medical home is a perfect fit for older adults who spend much more time interacting with the healthcare system. They want a medical home. (Erin Giovannetti, the National Committee for Quality Assurance)

The Patient-Centered Medical Home

HISTORY

In 1967, the American Academy of Pediatrics introduced the concept and term "medical home" as a description of a high-quality primary care provider that is accessible, family-centered, comprehensive, coordinated, compassionate, and culturally effective. Since the International Conference on Primary Health Care,[8] the World Health Organization,[9] the Institute of Medicine,[10] the American Academy of Family Physicians,[11] the American College of Physicians,[12] the

Patient-Centered Primary Care Collaborative,[13] and researcher Dr. Barbara Starfield have supported the medical home with impactful publications. In 2006, a group of large employers, including IBM and leading primary care physician associations, such as the American Osteopathic Association, the American Academy of Family Physicians, the American College of Physicians, and the American Academy of Pediatrics formed the Patient-Centered Primary Care Collaborative[14] to promote the patient-centered medical home. Today the collaborative has 1,000 multi-stakeholder members.

Since its passage in 2010, the Patient Protection Affordable Care Act has many provisions that have contributed to the expansion of patient-centered medical homes. The medical-home model exists around the world and continues to expand in the US. In their interview, Drs. Michael Barr and Erin Giovannetti describe the characteristics and outcomes of the patient-centered medical home. They also discuss the process of becoming recognized by the National Committee for Quality Assurance (NCQA).

> The patient-centered home model is better equipped to handle the complex care of patients with multiple chronic conditions who are more often older people.
>
> (Michael Barr, NCQA)

DR. ERIN R. GIOVANNETTI AND DR. MICHAEL S. BARR
NATIONAL COMMITTEE FOR QUALITY ASSURANCE

Erin Giovannetti is a Senior Research Scientist and Michael Barr is the Executive Vice President of the Quality Measurement and Research Group at the NCQA.[15]

The NCQA is committed to driving improvement in healthcare quality through research, development of evidence-based quality standards and performance measures, education and training, and advocacy. NCQA offers recognition, accreditation, and certification programs for a variety of care models and interventions. For the purpose of this book, we will examine the Patient-Centered Primary Care recognition program. To achieve recognition, primary care practices undergo a thorough multi-step review of 60 quality standards and report their annual quality and performance measures in more than 40 areas. The NCQA formula for improvement is: measure, analyze, improve, repeat.

In our research, we define excellent quality care as care that enables people to reach their goals even if their hemoglobin A1c is not precisely where their clinicians wanted to be. This requires a shift from care directed by the provider's goals to care directed by the patient's goals. (Erin Giovannetti)

Characteristics

Patient-centered medical homes (PCMHs) are also referred to as primary care medical homes and simply, medical homes. A medical home functions as a single point of care coordination and management for their patients. The care team consists of doctors, nurses, health educators, pharmacists, and other clinicians. The patient is included in all care decisions, and the care plan is individualized to the health profile and care preferences of the patient. In her interview, Erin described research that the NCQA is conducting into ways that health providers can better align care with the individual preferences of their patients. Medical homes also educate and encourage their patients to practice disease self-management and engage in prevention.

Patient-centered medical homes maintain the goal of improving safety and reducing the use of unnecessary, redundant, and low-value care. Medical homes use technology to improve efficiencies. The patient records are updated in real time and are accessible at all hours. Many practices use telehealth to connect to patients after hours.

The value-based reimbursement models in the US provide much incentive for providers to keep their patients out of the emergency departments (EDs) and hospitals. Access to care is a critical feature of the medical home. Patient-centered medical homes organize their scheduling in a way that enables them to provide same-day routine medical and urgent care. When patients do not have access to their primary care office, they are forced to go to the ED. Many of their health concerns are nonurgent. It is estimated that 30 to 50 percent of the ED visits in the US are for nonurgent needs.[16,17,18] This unnecessary care costs the US health system millions of dollars annually. We will delve more deeply into emergency care in our subsequent chapter, "Emergency Medicine and Hospital Care in the Home and Community."

Outcomes

Staff burnout[19] and turnover are detrimental to healthcare practices, both organizationally and financially. Michael Barr noted that physician and medical staff burnout decreases in practices that have become patient-centered medical homes. Group Health Cooperative in Seattle, Washington, realized a 20 percent decline in staff burnout one year after implementation of the medical home model.[20] The same practice saw higher patient satisfaction, quality, cost savings, and lower rates of provider burnout two years after their transformation to a medical home.[21] The Veterans Administration Health System also experienced lower burnout rates among their primary care employees after adopting the medical home model.[22] There is a plethora of evidence-based research on the NCQA website.[23] The research presents conclusive evidence that, when implemented correctly, recognized patient-centered medical homes improve access, quality (including patient satisfaction), and lower healthcare utilization and costs.

> Our recognition program represents the best thinking from a variety of stakeholders around the country, expert consensus, public opinion, and eight years of experience of the NCQA.
> (Michael Barr)

Recognition[24]

Michael Barr explained that to receive recognition, a practice must meet a specified number of standards that include:

- Patient-centered access;
- Team-based care;
- Population health management, care management, and support;
- Care coordination and care transitions;
- Performance management and quality improvement.

Within those standards there are six elements that represent the core of the medical home model. Practices must have all six of these elements to become recognized:

- Patient-centered appointment access;

- The Practice Team;[25]
- Use of data for population management purposes;
- Care planning and self-care support;
- Referral tracking and follow-up;
- Continual quality improvement.

Accreditation or recognition from NCQA gives practices the opportunity to demonstrate their commitment to quality, access, and patient satisfaction. To date, NCQA has recognized more than 11,000 patient-centered medical home primary care centers, representing 40 to 60 million patients. Some Veterans Health Administration (VHA) facilities are also recognized patient-centered medical homes.

When a veteran sees his primary care physician and complains of an ongoing hip problem, that physician can establish an immediate consult with an orthopedic doctor or a rehabilitation therapist in the same building. If those doctors need X-rays, lab tests, or diagnostic studies, they are done in house, usually the same day. If those studies indicate the need for surgery, a consult can be established immediately, with appropriate surgical clearance, and an operation conducted, all in the same facility, without a need to travel from one physician or facility to another. (Dr. Erik Langhoff)

DR. ERIK LANGHOFF
JAMES J. PETERS VA MEDICAL CENTER

Dr. Erik Langhoff is the Director of the James J. Peters VA Medical Center.[26]

The VHA is especially positioned to impact the health care of older adults because their patient population is older and has higher rates of comorbidity. Additionally, 25 to 30 percent have physical and/or other health issues that are related to their time in the military.

The VHA operates one of the largest healthcare systems in the world consisting of 152 hospitals, 800 community clinics, 126 nursing homes, and 35 domiciliaries. VHA hospitals and research facilities have provided at least some training for 60 percent of all medical residents in the US. The VHA is strongly committed to and supportive of research in developing groundbreaking health innovations such as the exoskeleton.[27] A comparison of hospital-level quality and patient experience data of non-VHA hospitals to VHA hospitals showed that the VHA outperformed on 6 of the 9 patient safety indicators. The VHA hospitals also exhibited better readmission and mortality rates.[28]

> Any discovery made in the Department of Veterans Affairs is ultimately shared with the entire world and benefits all of humanity.

Headquartered in Bronx, New York, the James J. Peters VA Medical Center serves an enrolled population of approximately 50,000 and an active user population of approximately 25,000 veterans. The James J. Peters VA Medical Center serves approximately 1,700 patients per day. The Center has more than 200 inpatient hospital beds and 68 nursing home beds and supports community outpatient clinics in Queens, Yonkers, and White Plains, New York.

> Here we can provide value over volume because, while we are tasked with being responsible stewards of the public money, our salary is not dependent on billing, and we do not chase profit.

Efficiency and Value-Based Care

Erik is originally from Denmark and is familiar with a well-functioning, government-run healthcare system. Erik launches and oversees continual multiple Lean Six Sigma projects in his commitment to streamlined efficiency. In his interview, Erik explained that billing does not drive the VHA because they are reimbursed by capitated payments. As mentioned in Chap. 1, with capitated payment arrangements, providers are paid a set amount per patient. This creates an inherent incentive to maintain an efficient system of care coordination that supports keeping their patient population healthy and out of the emergency department and hospital.

Access

Maintaining access to care is a vital component of the James J. Peters VA Medical Center. Increased access provides veterans with an alternative to going to the emergency department. A unique aspect of the VHA is the ability for physicians to work across state borders in person or via telemedicine. Physicians outside of the VHA must be licensed in the state where they practice. Erik and his colleagues are able to practice at all of the VHA facilities around the country. This is especially important because, at any moment, a specialist can be brought onto the care team remotely. The electronic health records of the veterans are also available at all VHA care facilities. If a veteran wishes to see a specialist in another state, they may, and their records will be available and up to date. Many VHA facilities also have evening and weekend walk-in clinics. By the end of the year, Erik plans to have the James J. Peters VA Medical Center offer same-day access to primary care and mental health services. The James J. Peters VA Medical Center is in the process of offering telemedicine from its emergency department so veterans can call and speak with an emergency department physician from home. The James J. Peters VA Medical Center also manages a telephone triage center that is available to approximately 900,000 veterans. The service will soon be available day and night. The Center provides home-based primary care and hospital-level care in a home for their older adults. Technology is an important aspect of the VHA care coordination.

Technology

In 1990 the VHA designed and built one of the most comprehensive electronic health records (EHR) in the world. At the time it was implemented, it was fully networked across the country in all VHA facilities. It was designed around patient care and coordination. More recently, the VHA upgraded their EHR to the same system that is used by the Department of Defense, thus capturing each veteran's health record from the time of service through the end of their lives. James J. Peters VA Medical Center was one of the first to provide telenephrology[29] and telekidney disease monitoring.

The Department of Veterans Affairs uses electronic prescription technology. Clinicians enter the prescription into the computer, and the medication is dispersed via mail by a centralized pharmacy. The patient also has the option of picking up their prescription in person. They use the same process for tests. The order for a test such as an x-ray is entered into the EHR. When the test is complete, it is automatically filed into the EHR. The complete real-time patient health record is available in one place at all times and in all locations. Demographic data is also included in the electronic health record and informs the care team about the social determinants that drive much of the health outcomes of their patients. Patients also have access to their EHR, including lab results, prescriptions, diagnoses, and contact information for their primary care doctor.

Barriers to Coordinated Primary Care

Changing an existing system of care delivery presents challenges that can be a strong barrier. It requires a full commitment by management and employees. Technology can act as a barrier when offices do not have electronic health systems or when those systems are not interoperable. Reimbursement policy can also act as a barrier to coordinated care. Reimbursements that are not value-based can dissuade providers from making the changes that are necessary to build an efficient, coordinated primary care practice.

It is our hope that patient-centered medical homes and other efficient coordinated primary care practices continue to spread nationally and globally to meet the needs of the older population and reduce healthcare costs.

As a continuation in our efforts to seek out cost-effective and person-centric models of care that reach into the home and community, we found four programs that have yielded impressive results in cost, quality, and health outcomes—including patient satisfaction. In the following chapter, we write about the importance of delivering acute and hospital-level care in the home of older adults and describe the DispatchHealth, Northwell Health, Call9, and Hospital at Home care models.

The full interviews can be found at this link: www.accessh.org/agingwell.

7

Emergency Medicine and Hospital Care in the Home and Community

The unsustainable course of healthcare spending in the United States has driven insurers to reward higher-quality, lower-cost care through value-based reimbursement agreements.[1] Providers are incentivized to keep patients well enough that they do not need to visit the emergency department (ED) or be admitted to the hospital. They are also incentivized to prevent hospital readmissions and ED bouncebacks of their patients.[2] The predominant contributing factors to readmissions and bouncebacks are little or no after-hour access to the care team and the lack of coordinated follow-up care after patients are discharged. Evidence shows that providing both acute and hospital-level care in the home and community can prevent or significantly lower the rates of hospital admissions, readmissions, emergency visits, and bouncebacks, resulting in better health outcomes, higher levels of patient satisfaction, and lower costs.

Emergency Department

The rapidly declining number of primary care physicians and geriatricians, combined with limited same-day and after-hour access, often makes the ED the only option for older people when they have a health need. Older adults use emergency care more than any other cohort and collectively make more than 20 million ED visits annually in the US,[3,4] accounting for 15 percent of all ED visits.[5] Overcrowding in the ED is already a cause for concern around the world[6,7,8] and can contribute to poor medical outcomes, including delays in treatment and diagnosis and adverse health events.[9,10,11,12] Without new systems to provide emergency care to the older population, overcrowding will only become worse because ED usage increases with age,[13] and the oldest old is the fastest growing age group in the world.[14,15] From 2010 to 2050, the number of those 85 and older in the US is expected to more than triple[16] and, by 2060, will represent one fourth of the population.[17]

Cost

One in five people in the US visits the ED annually.[18] The New England Healthcare Institute claims that unnecessary use of the ED is responsible for US$38 billion in annual healthcare costs.[19] An estimated 30 to 37 percent of all ED visits are considered nonurgent, meaning the patient could delay seeing a clinician for several hours without their health concern becoming worse.[20] Estimates show that more than 30 percent of Medicare beneficiaries who visit the ED and are not admitted to the hospital, could have been treated effectively in other settings.[21] Nearly one half of the residents in long-term care visit the ED annually, and most of those visits are considered avoidable.[22] From 2005 to 2010, nursing home residents made, on average, 1.8 ED visits annually in the US.[23] In 2005, unnecessary ED visits of nursing home residents insured by Medicare or Medicaid resulted in 314,000 possibly avoidable hospitalizations costing an estimated

US$2.6 billion.[24] Care in the ED is far more expensive than care in the ambulatory setting. One study estimated that if nonurgent cases were treated in urgent care centers or retail clinics, the health system would realize US$4.4 billion in cost savings annually.[25]

Risk for Older Adults

Emergency clinicians are rarely trained nor are they equipped to dedicate the additional time required to treat frail people with injuries and multiple chronic conditions. Emergency doctors quickly cure or treat episodic health events. Older adults are especially susceptible to adverse health events,[26] resulting from hospitalizations and emergency department visits.[27,28] They are at a higher risk of falling, developing infections, and experiencing dangerous medication interactions, missed diagnoses, and delirium.[29] To combat this risk and provide better care for older adults, some hospitals have added geriatric emergency departments. The first was built in 2008 in New Jersey, and today there are approximately 100 in the US.[30]

Cognitive Impairment in the ED

Those with cognitive impairment are at even greater risk for poor health outcomes in the ED.[31] Although 25 to 40 percent of older people who visit the ED have some form of cognitive impairment, it often goes undiagnosed.[32,33,34] Some estimates suggest that ED clinicians miss delirium 75 percent of the time and dementia 86.6 percent of the time.[35] This opens the door to medical error because patients are not able to provide an accurate medical history or description of their present health issue.[36] It also can contribute to inefficient, dangerous discharges because the patient might not be able to understand the discharge instructions. These patients are likely to bounce back to the ED for the same health concern.

Hospital

HOSPITALIZATIONS

People 65 and older use the hospital more than any other cohort. They account for 43 percent of hospital admissions in the US.[37]

Inpatient hospital services represent 23 percent of Medicare costs.[38] Medicare beneficiaries account for 46 percent of the aggregate hospital costs and 36 percent of the aggregate hospital stays.[39]

Readmission Costs

The cost of readmissions for Medicare patients alone is US$26 billion annually, and US$17 billion of that cost would not have occurred had the patient received the proper care during the first admission.[40] Twenty percent of older patients are readmitted to the hospital within a month of discharge.[41]

Risk for Older Adults

One in three Americans age 65 and older is living with multiple chronic conditions.[42] The rates of comorbidities increase with age and, as we mentioned, the oldest old represent the fastest growing population in the world. They are often frail with complex care needs and are more susceptible to adverse health events, including falls, infections, medication mismanagement, and medical error in the hospital and after discharge.[43] These events can lead to longer hospital stays and possibly result in death.

COGNITIVE IMPAIRMENT IN THE HOSPITAL

Patients who are admitted to the hospital after spending longer than 10 hours in the ED are at a higher risk of delirium.[44] The prevalence of delirium in the community is 1 to 2 percent, while 14 to 56 percent of hospitalized older patients experience it.[45] Delirium can lead to functional decline, loss of independence, and eventually death.[46] Patients who have dementia are 3 to 5 times more likely than others to develop delirium during and after a 30-day hospital stay. Episodes of delirium have shown to accelerate the rate of cognitive decline in patients with dementia.[47]

Hospitalization-associated disability (HAD) is the decreased ability to perform the activities of daily living at the time of discharge as compared to the baseline before admission.[48] HAD is the main cause of functional decline for older patients. More than 30 percent of patients over 70 experience HAD after being hospitalized for an acute illness.[49,50]

For every degree of increased dementia severity, as measured on the Global Deterioration Scale,[51] patients are 1.5 times more likely to experience delirium. Patients with dementia see longer hospitalization stays if they develop delirium[52] and are 25 percent less likely to have a full recovery from delirium than patients without dementia.[53]

The literature and demonstration projects suggest that it is important to design systems that can support the ability to treat people, especially older adults, in the home and community and keep them out of the hospital and ED whenever possible. One model of emergency care in the home and community that is receiving traction worldwide is paramedicine. Today there are paramedicine programs operational in approximately 20 states in the US.[54] We will share two examples of excellence.

We are an evolutionary extension of the emergency department. (Mark Prather)

DR. MARK PRATHER AND KEVIN RIDDLEBERGER
DISPATCHHEALTH

Mark Prather is the Chief Executive Officer, and Kevin Riddleberger is the Chief Strategy Officer of Colorado-based DispatchHealth. Dispatch Health provides acute health care in homes, offices, retirement communities, and skilled nursing facilities.[55] The DispatchHealth leadership is comprised of technology innovators and seasoned emergency medical clinicians. More than 60 percent of their patients are 65 and older and are insured by Medicare, Medicaid, or Medicare Advantage health plans.

When a person requests medical care for an acute medical condition with DispatchHealth via phone, website, or mobile app, they are connected with a DispatchHealth clinician to triage the call. During the initial call, the DispatchHealth clinicians gather further information about the patient and their acute medical condition to determine whether the person can be treated safely at home or their place of employment. If the person can be treated at home or work, a DispatchHealth team is deployed. If the person needs hospital care, they send an ambulance.

Documenting impediments to care is a new level of care coordination. (Mark Prather)

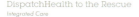

DispatchHealth to the Rescue
Integrated Care

DispatchHealth is positioned to work as an extension of the existing care team to allow for improved communication, improved clinical data exchange and comprehensive care coordination to improve patient outcomes and decrease total cost of care.

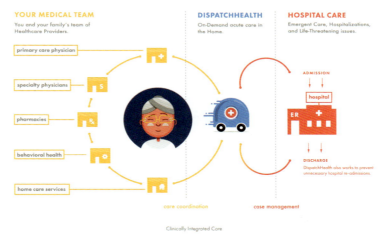

Source: DispatchHealth

The DispatchHealth team has a higher level of clinical capabilities than most urgent care centers. The care team includes an emergency medical technician and an emergency department-trained board-certified nurse practitioner or a physician assistant. The average length of the DispatchHealth home or office visit is just under an hour. This is notable because rarely, if ever, does a medical team in the ED have almost an hour to spend with one patient. During and after the visit, communication is established and coordination of care is performed with the patient's existing primary care or specialty care medical team. DispatchHealth clinicians also perform a social determinants of health assessment of the patient's home to identify other potential health risks or impediments to care, including: lack of access to transportation for follow-up care, fall hazards, medication management issues, access to food, ability to perform activities of daily living, and availability of social support. The team shares this information with the primary care team and/or care coordinators so they can connect the patient to necessary social supports to prevent readmissions or bouncebacks and improve the patient's ongoing health. This preventative benefit is only possible because the care team is in the patient's home.

Thirty to forty percent of what used to be done in the hospital can be done in the home for a fraction of the cost. (Mark Prather)

A home or office visit from the DispatchHealth team is approximately eight to ten times less expensive than a visit to the ED. These cost savings caught the attention of public and private insurers who reimburse DispatchHealth to serve their beneficiaries. DispatchHealth now operates in seven markets across the country and works with large commercial, Managed Medicaid, and Medicare Advantage plans to be an in-network provider in the markets it offers medical services. Those insurers include Medicare, Medicaid, Tricare, Anthem, Blue Cross Blue Shield, United Healthcare, Aetna, Humana, and Cigna.

Our goal is to produce outcome-based medicine, not more medicine. We do not need more care; we need integrated care. (Mark Prather)

CARE COORDINATION ACROSS THE CONTINUUM

Mark and Kevin described the ability of the DispatchHealth team to access patient electronic medical records through the health information exchange. When DispatchHealth clinicians visit a patient, they have full knowledge of their health profile and current medications.

After providing care, the medical team updates the health profile in real time for the primary care doctor. The rest of the patient's medical team has the same up-to-date information. The exchange also enables DispatchHealth to follow their patients' progress by monitoring the activity on the exchange to determine whether a patient bounces back to the ED with a similar health concern. This an important quality measure used by DispatchHealth.

> If we are going to create a better system, we need to eliminate redundant care. (Mark Prather)

BOUNCEBACK RATES

The newer reimbursement policy in the US rewards higher value and better outcomes. Bouncebacks are expensive and cause patient suffering. They also imply that the care or follow-up care was not adequate during the first health event. Each patient visited by the DispatchHealth team receives a phone checkup three days after treatment. Mark mentioned that the national average bounceback rate for emergency departments is 1 in 5 or 20 percent. The bounceback rate for DispatchHealth patients is 6 percent. This represents an exponential savings for insurers because the cost for the initial visit is eight to ten times lower and avoiding a bounceback is 100 percent savings of a follow-up ED visit, hospitalization, and possibly an ambulance charge. Receiving coordinated care and avoiding an

ED visit and bounceback also contribute substantially to patient satisfaction and well-being.

PATIENT SATISFACTION

Patient satisfaction is a quality measure that is becoming ever more important because it is the core of patient-centered care. DispatchHealth uses the Net Promoter Score to measure patient satisfaction. Their score ranges from 93 to 95 as compared to the industry average score of 30.

We have flipped the model of access to acute care.

(Kevin Riddleberger)

ACCESS

Another quality measure that is receiving much attention because of the high rates of ED usage is access to same-day or after-hour care. DispatchHealth services are available to patients every day of the week from 8 am to 10 pm. DispatchHealth care is also more accessible because patients do not have to leave their homes and wait in an emergency department for treatment.

SENIOR LIVING COMMUNITIES

DispatchHealth has developed partnerships with home health agencies, senior living communities, primary care providers, specialty practices, hospice and palliative care providers, nurse advice lines, EMS agencies, and health systems. In 2017, DispatchHealth completed 6,834 patient visits to individuals aged 65 and older. Of these visits, only 8 percent were transferred to the hospital. The estimated cost savings from these patients avoiding usage of the 911 system and the ED in 2017 was US$12.6 million. The estimates do not take into account the thousands of avoidable hospitalizations that DispatchHealth likely prevented. DispatchHealth is projected to produce well over US$20 million in cost savings in 2017. As DispatchHealth continues to grow and move into new markets, we can only imagine the cost savings will continue to grow as well.

The beneficial outcomes are not only financial. The well-being of older adults who avoid the physical and emotional strain of the ambulance, ED, and possibly hospital admission cannot be underestimated. Additionally, home health agencies are rewarded with better CMS star ratings[56] for lowering their rates of unplanned ED visits or hospitalizations.

Kevin and Mark identified the healthcare issues prevalent today that DispatchHealth is positioned to address. They include:

- 4.4 billion Medicare dollars are wasted in unnecessary emergency care annually;

- 37 percent of emergency department visits are estimated to be unnecessary;
- More than 4 billion dollars are spent each year on potentially avoidable ED visits and hospital admissions by residents in long-term care;
- Medicaid expansion contributed to a 40 percent increase in emergency department visits;
- The US health system is in need of 50,000 more primary care physicians;
- 17–25 percent of 911 transports are unnecessary or inappropriate.

Since the interview with Kevin and Mark, DispatchHealth has continued to expand its services across the country. It now operates in Denver, Colorado; Colorado Springs, Colorado; Phoenix, Arizona; Richmond, Virginia; Las Vegas, Nevada; Houston, Texas; and Oklahoma City, Oklahoma. They plan to be in 10 markets by the end of 2018 with projections to see more than 50,000 patients and save the healthcare delivery system more than US$80 million in unnecessary ambulance trips, ED visits, and hospitalizations.

Another community paramedicine program that has shown to reduce ED visits dramatically is based out of Northwell Health in Long Island, New York.

DR. KRISTOFER SMITH
NORTHWELL HEALTH SOLUTIONS

Kristofer Smith is the Senior Vice President of the Office of Population Health Management and the Medical Director for Northwell Health Solutions, the largest integrated health delivery system in New York State. He is also an Associate Professor in the Department of Medicine at the Hofstra Northwell School of Medicine.

We detailed the house calls or home-based palliative care program of Northwell Health in Chap. 3. Northwell Health trained a clinical team to use their large fleet of ambulances to serve patients in the house calls program. When a patient or family member calls for urgent care, the health situation is triaged. If there is a need to escalate care, a doctor is called to determine if the person can be treated at home. If the patient is treated at home, the average arrival time for the care team is 23 minutes. The paramedicine team contacts the doctor with the initial evaluation results and the team determines the next course of action together.

At the time of his interview, Kristofer Smith noted that they had conducted more than 1,100 paramedicine visits in 2.5 years. In those years, 77 percent of the patients were treated at home as compared the industry average of less than 10 percent. A patient survey revealed that, without the paramedicine service, 86 percent of the patients would have gone to the ED. In that period, Northwell Health realized an estimated US$3.8 million of cost savings by avoiding ED visits, ambulance transports, and hospital admissions.

LATE LIFE PLANNING

The Northwell Health paramedicine program is unique because it is part of the care continuum for existing older patients with multiple chronic conditions. This means that the urgent care team is aware of the patients' individual preferences and goals for care and are able to honor those preferences. If a typical ambulance in another town visits a frail older patient, they will likely bring the person to the hospital where he or she will likely receive invasive, extensive, and costly care. The older individual may not even want such care if asked. The emergency medical technicians would not know that possibly the patient would prefer to remain at home and be kept comfortable and out of pain. Honoring the care goals and priorities of the patient is another important measure of patient-centeredness.

BARRIERS TO IMPLEMENTATION

The main barriers to implementation of acute care in the home include reimbursements that do not pay for the services, difficulty in reorganizing existing health systems, and changing the stakeholder and institutional view of where emergency medicine is best delivered. Home can be defined as the place where a person resides, which includes retirement communities and skilled nursing facilities.

ACUTE CARE DELIVERY IN SKILLED NURSING HOMES

One half of nursing home hospitalizations have been deemed unnecessary,[57] including hospitalizations that occurred in the last year of life.[58] The health system costs and detrimental effects of these hospitalizations on the patient's quality of life are dramatic.

As of 2000, an estimated 70 percent of nursing home residents were living with cognitive impairment (CI).[59] Because the incidence increases with age, as the oldest old population grows, so will the number of nursing home residents with CI. Those residents are more likely to experience a preventable ED visit and hospitalizations.[60,61]

The innovation behind Call9 is straight forward: Why take a nursing home resident to the hospital when you really do not have to? (Timothy Peck)

DR. TIMOTHY PECK, XIAOSONG MU, AND GARRETT GLEESON CALL9

Timothy Peck and XiaoSong Mu are the founders of Call9 and Garrett Gleeson is Chief of Staff. Timothy Peck was a former emergency department doctor who, with a technologically sophisticated team, built Call9 to fill the gap between care in the emergency department and the nursing home. Call9 provides around-the-clock acute and follow-up care in skilled nursing homes. This enables the residents to avoid a visit to the ED and risk being hospitalized. They also provide palliative care. As we have detailed in Chap. 4, without access to palliative and hospice care, patients are forced into what some refer to as "assault and battery care" (the cycle from ED, to hospital, and back to skilled nursing) throughout the last years of life. This cycle is costly and causes patient suffering, often without any beneficial health outcomes. To our knowledge, there is no other provider of around-the-clock emergency care delivered in nursing homes in the US.

> I wanted to find a way to fill the need gap between nursing home care and emergency care that was more patient centered, had better outcomes, and was less costly. (Timothy Peck)

WHY NURSING HOME RESIDENTS ARE SENT TO THE ED

Timothy spent time living in a nursing home to understand why residents were sent to the emergency department. He boiled down the issue to three main contributing factors:

- The nurse-to-patient ratio (at best, 1 to 20) does not give nurses the time to attend to acute medical events;
- The nursing home staff does not have the diagnostic capabilities needed for acute care;
- Physicians and other high-level clinicians are not available after hours.

HOW THE CALL9 MODEL WORKS

Call9 places emergency and geriatric-trained clinical care specialists in nursing homes around the clock. The specialists are trained on a continuing basis in a skill set that is different from a nurse, and that has a geriatric component. When a patient in one of the skilled nursing homes that Call9 serves has an adverse health event, the Call9 clinical specialist is at the bedside within minutes. This is in contrast to the other option of waiting for an ambulance, traveling to the ED, and waiting in line at the, often over crowded, ED for care. The specialist immediately begins a series of diagnostic tests and contacts the emergency physician who is available around the clock virtually. All of the electronic medical records, patient workflow, telemetry, and lab and diagnostic results are uploaded in real time online to the patient dashboard that the physician has on his or her screen. Together the physician, via tablet, and specialists determine whether the patient can be treated at home or should be transported to the ED.

FOLLOW-UP CARE

The Call9 team provides follow-up care for their patients that usually lasts two to three days or longer if the situation warrants. Internal medical physicians oversee the follow-up care that is also tracked in detail by the clinical care specialist via technology.

We have embedded a light model of an emergency department in the nursing homes we serve. (Timothy Peck)

Honoring the Care Priorities and Advanced Directives

Call9 clinical care specialists maintain close and ongoing relationships with the residents and their families. Together they build a late life care plan that is centered around the well-being and priorities of the resident. The specialists maintain a continued presence throughout the care continuum, from palliative to hospice care. This coordinated, person-centric model enables people to be at home and not in the hospital when they die.

In his interview, Timothy shared an example of how a patient was able to die with dignity at home (in the nursing home) with her husband by her side. During a teleconference, one of their physicians explained to the husband that his wife was likely to die soon. After the husband's initial shock and fear, he made the choice to spend their remaining time together in the nursing home rather than going to the hospital. It was the couple's 65th wedding anniversary. They spent their remaining time quietly together until she passed away. In itself this story represents patient-centered care at its best because the goals of the patient and the family override heroic medical interventions.

An unseen aspect of the above case is how these moments affect the team of Call9. Engineers who design the complex technology behind the scenes are privy to the human aspect of their mission that can facilitate dignity in death for their patients and peace and comfort for their families. These situations also are more fulfilling to physicians and the rest of the care team who have built caring relationships with their patients and families.

Population Health Data

Call9 is capturing extensive data on patients experiencing an acute health event. This aggregated specialized data could prove useful in population health management in the future and is used to direct the Call9 practices and resource allocation.

Eighty percent of the patients we see would still go to the emergency department if we did not keep treating them after the original event. (Timothy Peck)

Clinical and Cost Outcomes

The Call9 business model is built on providing value-based care. Call9 is reimbursed mostly by the savings to the insurer. Call9 has reimbursement arrangements with most of the large insurers in the area they serve. Eighty percent of the residents seen by Call9 avoid transport to the ED and potential subsequent hospitalization. An independent economics firm reviewed the Call9 outcome data and determined that based on hospital avoidance, Call9 was saving each nursing home US$8 million per year.

Another program that addresses the concerns of insurers who are focused on reducing the number of hospitalizations and the resulting cost and subpar health outcomes is the one that delivers hospital-level care in the home. Hospital at Home and "Hospital in the Home" programs are operational in Australia, the United Kingdom, Italy, New Zealand, and Israel. In North America, Hospital at Home services are available in:

- Some Veterans Affairs Medical Centers;
- Presbyterian Health Services in Albuquerque, New Mexico;
- Cedars Sinai Medical Center in Los Angeles, California;
- Geisinger Health Systems in Pennsylvania;

- Cleveland Clinic in Cleveland, Ohio;
- Brigham and Women's Hospital in Boston, Massachusetts, and
- Mt. Sinai in Toronto, Canada.

Mount Sinai in New York is conducting a CMS innovation demonstration project of Hospital at Home through the Icahn School of Medicine in New York.[62] The project will collect data from the demonstration with the goal of making Hospital at Home a reimbursable service through a bundled payment agreement.[63]

Hospital care at home has shown to reduce mortality and readmission rates, improve patient and family satisfaction, and result in shorter length of stays and fewer complications at a lower cost.[64,65]

I see the hospital of the future as one large intensive care unit that provides high tech procedures. All other care should be provided outside of the hospital setting. (Dr. Bruce Leff)

DR. BRUCE LEFF
HOSPITAL AT HOME

Bruce Leff is a professor of medicine at the Johns Hopkins University School of Medicine where he directs the Center for Transformative Geriatric Research.

Hospital at Home is a 20-year evidence-based project of Bruce and his team at the Johns Hopkins University School of Medicine. Hospital at Home care begins when a person arrives at the emergency department.

The clinical team conducts an assessment using the checklist of criterion to determine whether a patient qualifies for hospital care at home. The criterion also helps to identify frail older patients who are more likely to decompensate in the hospital setting.

Physicians and nurses visit the patients at varying rates depending on the need. The most common diagnoses of patients treated at home include pneumonia, reoccurring congestive heart failure, deep vein thrombosis, cellulitis, pulmonary embolism, urinary tract infection, nausea, vomiting, and dehydration.

Bruce explained that Hospital at Home can be adapted to other forms of care in the home. Mount Sinai is considering moving sub-acute rehabilitation into the home when appropriate as a result of the shortage of skilled nursing hospital beds in Manhattan. It is a win-win proposition because patients want care in the home and the provider realizes cost savings. Bruce expects that, going forward, as care and reimbursements become less siloed, Hospital at Home will be adapted to other areas of care.

> If you are responsible for the total bill of health care and you own all the assets of health care, keeping people out of the hospitals makes good economic sense.

COST

Bruce described that single-payer systems[66] and managed care organizations[67] have inherent economic incentives to provide high-quality care at a lower cost because they are the payer and the payee. These incentives lead to the early proliferation of Hospital at Home beginning with managed care organizations and the Veterans Administration. Bruce noted that Hospital at Home costs 20 to 30 percent less than a hospitalization and results in significantly better health outcomes, including shorter hospital stays, fewer lab and diagnostic tests, and slightly lower hospital readmission and mortality rates. Today's evolving reimbursement landscape, which emphasizes value, promises to drive more systemic uptake by hospitals in the US.

Providing hospital care at home also includes avoiding the societal costs of building new hospitals in countries with government-funded health care. Bruce explained that it costs approximately US$2 million to capitalize one hospital bed, which means that a 500-bed hospital costs approximately US$1 billion for the building alone.

Hospital at Home is patient-centric, community-based care.

PATIENT SATISFACTION

The Hospital at Home team conducted studies to explore people's feelings about receiving hospital care at home. The feedback was positive—even people in their late 90s reported that they prefer to receive care at home when possible. Bruce noted poor communication is the main driver of malpractice lawsuits. He also noted that having a care team visit the home and meet with the family forms a more person-centered relationship with better communication. Patients and their families report a higher satisfaction level with such individualized care.

There is still a dominant bias toward facility-based care.

BARRIERS TO IMPLEMENTATION

Reimbursements still remain a barrier to implementation of Hospital at Home. Possibly the CMS innovation demonstrations will make Hospital at Home reimbursable in the future. Since our interview, Bruce mentioned that the Hospital at Home had submitted a proposal to the Physician-Focused Payment Model Technical Advisory Committee[68] (PTAC) to recommend that CMS reimburse for Hospital at Home. We sincerely hope that will happen.

Changing long-standing beliefs and habits remains an additional barrier to Hospital at Home, DispatchHealth, Northwell Health, and Call9. For years facility-based care has been considered the gold standard and the only safe option by providers and patients alike. We hope that time, reimbursement policy, and evidence will challenge those beliefs and expand to include emergency care in the home—wherever home may be.

Our next chapter is about supporting those with dementia and their caregivers. We write about an intervention that enables caregivers of a person with dementia to keep their loved one at home for, on average, one year longer. We also write about other programs that support the well-being of caregivers and those with dementia for whom they care. The need to support caregivers cannot be underestimated. Caregivers are often referred to as the silent army: without formal and informal caregivers, the global burden of supporting the aging population would become nothing short of a crisis.

The full interviews referenced in this chapter can be found at this link: www.accessh.org/agingwell.

8

Support for Those Living with Dementia and Their Caregivers

In 2015, an estimated 46.8 million people in the world were living with dementia.[1] That number is expected to nearly double every 20 years, and by 2050 is projected to reach 131.5 million.[2] Forty-nine percent of the new dementia cases are seen in Asia, 25 percent in Europe, 18 percent in the Americas, and 8 percent in Africa.[3] In 2015 the global costs of dementia were estimated to be US$818 billion, which represents a 35.4 percent increase since 2010.[4] In the United States, the annual cost of dementia care is estimated at US$159 billion to US$215 billion[5] and is projected to grow to US$1.1 trillion by 2050.[6] Most dementia care costs can be attributed to long-term care and not medical care. Institutional and informal home care is responsible for 75 to 84 percent of the total costs of dementia.[7]

Caregiving

Dementia is one of the leading causes of disability and dependency for older adults worldwide.[8,9] Approximately one half of those in need of caregiving have dementia.[10] In the next decade, the US will need 1.3 million more paid caregivers.[11] The approaching need, combined with the caregiver shortage that already exists, will present care challenges that could place an even larger burden on the shoulders of informal caregivers.

Informal caregivers are family or relatives, mostly female,[12] who provide unpaid care and support. Informal caregivers face financial, emotional, and physical strain. They are more likely to experience physical health problems, depression, and anxiety.[13] Some are forced to leave the workforce. Sixty-eight percent of family caregivers in the US reported that they had to make work accommodations, including retiring, working part-time, or taking time off.[14]

Informal caregivers provide the bulk of dementia care.[15] Thirty-four percent of the informal caregivers in the US are 64 or older.[16] Dementia care exceeds the demands of many other chronic conditions. Those with dementia require more assistance with activities of daily living[17] and can exhibit emotional behaviors that are unfamiliar and difficult to manage. Most informal caregivers are not prepared, nor do they have the training for the tasks needed to provide the necessary care.[18,19]

In 2010, of the adults age 70 and older who received informal care, an estimated 3.6 million had cognitive impairment that was likely dementia.[20] In 2016 informal caregivers in the US provided 18.2 billion hours valued at more than US$230 billion.[21] More than 40 percent of the costs of dementia care globally can be attributed to informal caregivers.[22] This is a valuable cost savings to public and private healthcare insurers. With this knowledge, insurers and managed healthcare systems have a vested interest in supporting informal caregivers. Support for informal caregivers has shown to improve well-being for the caregiver and the person living with dementia.[23] Caregiver support has also shown to delay institutional care.[24]

There is no drug yet available that can prevent or cure dementia, but psychosocial interventions have been proved to have a significant positive impact on persons with dementia and their caregivers. (Dr. Mary S. Mittelman)

DR. MARY S. MITTELMAN
NYU CAREGIVER INTERVENTION

Mary Mittelman is the director of the Psychosocial Research and Support Program at the Center for Cognitive Neurology at New York University. She is also a research professor at the Department of Psychiatry and the Department of Rehabilitation Medicine at NYU School of Medicine.

Along with an expert team, Mary developed the NYU Caregiver Intervention in her lab at the NYU School of Medicine. The evidence-based intervention provides psychological support to the informal caregiver for someone living with dementia. The intervention includes two individual counseling sessions, four family counseling sessions, weekly support groups, and "ad hoc" counseling available by phone to the family and caregiver. Counselors offer support to the caregiver and the family throughout the course of the caregiving journey and up to two years after.

Everyone is interested in research on drug trials and how drugs can improve cognitive function. I think that we should be equally concerned with well-being and quality-of-life for those with dementia, their caregiver, and their family.

The initial research of the intervention began with a randomized control trial in 1987. The caregivers in the treatment group experienced positive outcomes, including fewer symptoms of depression, increased satisfaction with support from family, less reactivity to the person for whom they were caring, and improved physical health. Another notable outcome was that the caregivers in the treatment group were able to keep their family member at home for, on average, one and half years longer than those in the control group.

The intervention has been well documented in peer-reviewed journals.[25,26,27,28] Since the initial research, there have been many well-documented translations of the intervention in the US.[29,30,31,32,33] Other translations were conducted in the United Kingdom, Israel, and Australia. In 2015, New York State Governor Andrew M. Cuomo granted NYU Langone Medical Center US$7.5 million to launch the Family Support Program, making the NYU Caregiver Intervention available to residents throughout New York City who are caring for someone with dementia. Mary and her team are planning to serve 600 caregivers annually in this program.

In her interview, Mary compared the intervention to a cake. Leaving out an important ingredient or changing the timing or dosage will not result in the cake you had planned. Mary explained that the most important component of the intervention is family involvement. The ability of the caregivers in the treatment group to keep their family member home for a year and a half longer than those in the control group was due to their social support, emotional support from family and friends, assistance from family and friends, and the number of people the caregiver felt close to. Those who have tried to replicate the intervention without the family piece have not realized the successful outcomes.

An unsuccessful replication led Mary and her team to write a book entitled *Counseling the Alzheimer's Caregiver: A Resource for Healthcare Professionals.*[34] Mary and her team also decided to develop an online training course to ensure the validity of future replications. The training incorporates videos of case studies along with text and video commentary. Today, anyone in the world looking to offer the NYU Caregiver Intervention has the tools to do so.

Mary and her team were concerned that family members who wish to participate might have issues with traffic and transportation, varying hours of availability, or could live in another state or even country. Those concerns led to the creation of a videoconferencing version of the intervention.

> It is time that insurers understand the importance of treating the caregiver.

When a caregiver feels lower levels of stress and depression, they make less use of the healthcare system for their own needs. This represents a cost savings to the insurer. The other substantial cost savings results from the ability of the caregiver to keep the family member home for a year and a half longer. Mary is convinced that the intervention should be reimbursed by insurance. Recently there was a letter circulating in the Senate that explained the importance of caregiver support. That letter mentions the New York University Caregiver Intervention. It is our hope that the increasing awareness of the value of supporting the caregiver of someone with dementia will influence insurers and managed care providers in the US and healthcare systems worldwide.

Those living with dementia, their caregivers, and their families benefit from services, education, and supports. Professionals of all disciplines who work with people living with dementia need dementia-specific training to better serve their clientele (See Fig. 8.1).

This is our time to care.

Every mother. Every father.
Every child. Every New Yorker.

It takes a certain kind to
rise to the challenge.

The courageous kind.
The resilient kind.
The loving kind.
Our kind.

We are CaringKind.

The Heart of Alzheimer's Caregiving.

Figure 8.1 CaringKind entrance welcome

JED A. LEVINE
CARINGKIND

Jed Levine is the Executive Vice President and Director of Programs and Services at CaringKind in New York City.

For more than 30 years, CaringKind has been providing free education, support, assistance, and training for those living with early stage dementia and their caregivers. Approximately 15,000 people, including trainees, volunteers, support group members, and those seeking other services, walk through the CaringKind doors each year. CaringKind also trains and educates professionals who serve those living with dementia. They offer approximately 90 support groups that are held throughout New York City in community centers, hospitals, churches, synagogues, nursing homes, and community-based organizations. CaringKind also operates a 24-hour telephone hotline that receives approximately 750 to 900 calls each month. The employees manning the call line provide comfort and connect callers to additional supportive services.

We recognize that the person receiving the diagnosis and their family are in a lot of emotional pain. Sometimes they are paralyzed with fear and the feeling of helplessness. Most people do not know where to begin. If they call us for information and direction, they also receive validation for what they are experiencing. We assure them that they do not have to face the challenge alone. (Jed A. Levine)

Mission

In his interview, Jed explained that the funding for CaringKind is approximately 85 percent philanthropic and 15 percent governmental and other sources. Many of the CaringKind board members view their service as a personal mission because the disease has touched their family or friends. A personal connection to dementia can unite a group or organization through a shared mission. With the growing rates of dementia, it is likely everyone will eventually share this personal connection.

Minorities and Dementia

Jed mentioned that CaringKind was making strides in their efforts to reach minority communities. When Jed joined CaringKind, he was dedicated to making sure that anyone in need of CaringKind's services would be supported by someone who speaks their language and understands their culture. Chinese immigrants represent the second largest group of foreign citizens in New York, and they are projected to eventually take first place over Dominican born residents.[35] CaringKind has a full-time outreach manager in the Chinese community to raise the visibility of the disease and encourage people to engage with the supports available to them. CaringKind has made such strides within the Asian community that they have hired a full-time social worker to support the Chinese families seeking assistance. They have also hired a trainer who speaks Cantonese and Mandarin to teach workshops and training to families and caregivers. CaringKind has made the same inroads with the Latino Community.

African Americans are more likely to develop Alzheimer's than Whites, with estimates ranging widely from 14 to 100 percent.[36] They are also twice as likely to develop late-onset Alzheimer's and are less likely to seek a diagnosis of their conditions.[37] Jed noted that it took CaringKind longer to establish trust within the African American community than any other communities they serve. It took the outreach manager five years to convince the African American communities to trust that CaringKind would be there to support them. Now African Americans attend dementia-specific legal and financial workshops and use the social work and supportive services at CaringKind.

The Early Stage Center

The Early Stage Center fills the gap between those who cannot function independently in programs designed for people without dementia and those who have not yet progressed to the stage of needing adult day programs. It also fills the need for social interaction in a safe and accepting environment. Support groups enable participants to share their fears and grief. Jed mentioned that participants create empowering connections through their shared experiences. They laugh and they cry but leave feeling supported. Many participants have not yet told their family or friends that they have been diagnosed. Jed noted that it is a powerful experience to hear people tell their story publicly for the first time.

The Early Stage Center connects their members to art museums, historical museums, botanical gardens, and musical performances. The events are socially and culturally enriching experiences. Jed mentioned that music and art have a special connection in the brain of those living with dementia. The Early Center also has a variety of programs, including meditation, yoga, art, film, theater, and photography. The photography program is popular because the photos are often stunning and are taken by both experienced and novice photographers. Geri Taylor, a participant of the photography program, allowed a *New York Times* reporter to document her journey with Alzheimer's for two years.[38] Providing supports and services for someone living with dementia is important, but it is also essential to train the healthcare workforce serving those living with dementia.

Workforce Training

One cannot underestimate the importance of training the healthcare workforce in dementia care and communication. The US is already lacking in a workforce trained in dementia, and the shortage of physicians, nurses, and social workers is expected to continue to rise.[39] CaringKind offers dementia training to professionals, including homecare workers, certified nursing assistance, and people working in long-term care. They also provide education to nursing and social work schools. CaringKind has an education program for chaplains who wish to learn more about dementia so they can better serve the spiritual needs of their congregants with dementia.

Financial and Legal Planning

Jed described that, in the US, legal and financial planning is important for those with dementia and their families. It is not uncommon for one spouse to spend down their savings and even lose their home to pay for long-term care for their spouse with dementia. This leaves the surviving spouse financially insecure. It is estimated that 20 percent of those caring for someone with dementia go hungry because they cannot afford enough food.[40] In other cases, the spouse who handles the finances is the one with dementia, making them vulnerable to scams and risky financial decisions. CaringKind connects their clients with experts in these areas for financial counseling. CaringKind also connects families to attorneys for guidance in durable power of attorney and estate planning.

Respite

Respite provides caregivers a temporary break while someone else assumes the care responsibilities. Respite varies in duration from an hour to run errands to several days to take a vacation. Respite can result in lower levels of caregiver burnout and better care for the person living with dementia. CaringKind offers respite services to their members. Social workers also help members to design a long-term care plan with scheduled respite periods.

Palliative Care Pilot Program

CaringKind is dedicated to raising the awareness of palliative care for those living with dementia. They conducted three pilot programs of the Beatitudes Campus Comfort Matters™ palliative care model[41] in three nursing homes in New York, including the Isabella Geriatric Center, The New Jewish Home, and Cobble Hill Health Center. The pilot involved a two-year training and integration plan, with the goal of certifying the three providers in Comfort Matters. Jed is convinced that this model can transform the lives of those living in residential care.

Wandering

Sixty percent of those with dementia will wander, and all people with memory challenges are at risk for wandering.[42] Some claim that dementia wandering is driven by desire for those living with dementia to return to their younger days.[43] If they were ranchers, they might wish to go outside each morning to check on the cows, and if they were homemakers, they might wish to leave to drive their children to and from school and activities. In Chap. 2 we examined person-centered methods to alleviate the desire of residents in long-term care to wander. Prevention may be more difficult with untrained caregivers in the home. When the person living with dementia wanders and becomes disoriented or confused, he or she will not be able to find their way home. This elopement can present many dangers for the person with dementia and much stress for their families and caregivers. CaringKind has a low-tech, high-impact program for finding people with dementia after they have wandered.

ELIZABETH BRAVO SANTIAGO
CARINGKIND

Elizabeth Bravo Santiago is the Director of the MedicAlert® NYC Wanderer's Safety Program at CaringKind.[44]

The MedicAlert® NYC Wanderer's Safety Program is a collaboration between the New York City Police Department, the New York City Office of Emergency Management, the New York City Department for the aging, the Port Authority, the Transit Authority, the New York City Police Department Housing Bureau, other responders, and CaringKind. The mission of the program is to locate people with dementia who have gone missing. Approximately 21 searches arise through the MedicAlert® NYC Wanderer's Safety Program monthly. Elizabeth also coordinates with the police department's Silver Alert system, which is an alert for missing people who are 65 or older. Elizabeth assists in finding an average of 40 people each month through the two programs. In her 13 years directing the program, all but two people were found alive.

How the Program Works

When a person has wandered, a family member or caregiver calls 911. The police department takes a report and sends it to the Missing Persons detective unit. The detective then visits the home of the missing person to learn more information from their family and/or caregiver. The detective canvasses the appropriate area and alerts the other police departments about the special missing person. They also contact MedicAlert®, who contacts Elizabeth. The wanderer does not have to be one of the 25,000 people who are enrolled in the program through CaringKind. Elizabeth reaches out to the incident reporter, who is often the caregiver, to gain additional information and to provide emotional support. She explains that it is not the fault of the caregiver and that she understands the challenge of caring for someone with dementia. During her conversations with the caregiver or family, Elizabeth learns the patterns that the wanderer exhibited in the past that provide clues as to where he or she has gone. Elizabeth then posts the missing person bulletin on social media. Elizabeth noted that many wanderers forget their names and phone numbers. Sometimes female wanderers will revert to their maiden name. In anticipation of the confusion, Elizabeth collects all possible options from the family and forwards the information to hospitals and police departments.

> I play the role of advocate and provide support
> for the caregiver.

Elizabeth gives the caregiver or family member her mobile phone number and remains an around-the-clock source of reassurance throughout the search process. Elizabeth mentioned that she reminds the caregiver or family member to take care of him or herself during the stressful time and to ask friends and family for support. The average length of time a wanderer is lost ranges from 48 to 72 hours.

I treat caregivers as though they were my family members.

MedicAlert® is a national database that registers the health history and contact information of those enrolled. Healthcare and law enforcement professionals are trained to recognize the bracelets and necklaces. Elizabeth encourages all of the CaringKind clients to enroll in the MedicAlert® program. CaringKind will occasionally help with the cost of enrollment when needed (See Fig. 8.2).

The MedicAlert® NYC Wanderer's Safety Program is also useful in the event of a disaster. Elizabeth shared an example of the large explosion that occurred one day in New York City. Police immediately called Elizabeth to determine whether any of the residents near the explosion had dementia so they could locate them and make sure they were safe. Elizabeth stayed in touch with the police and the family until the people with dementia were located.

Figure 8.2 MedicAlert® bracelet and necklace

Case Studies

Caregivers of those enrolled in the program also wear a MedicAlert®
bracelet or necklace with information of the person living with
dementia. One day, after visiting the Veterans Administration Hospital,
a husband with dementia and his wife boarded the bus home. The wife
was exhausted and fell asleep during the bus ride. When she awoke, her
husband was gone. The wife was in a panic when she approached the
bus driver to ask whether he had seen her husband leave the bus. Her
English was broken at best. She gave her necklace to the driver who
then knew to call the police and report the man missing. The husband
was found at a local hospital before the day ended.

MedicAlert® is an international program, which was useful to Elizabeth when a person with dementia from New York City walked into a
beauty parlor in Jamaica. He told the owner he was waiting for his wife,
but when it was time to close the shop, the owner became concerned.
She noticed his bracelet and contacted MedicAlert® who then contacted Elizabeth. The family had notified Elizabeth that they would be
in Jamaica on vacation so she was prepared. Elizabeth called the family
and they retrieved their dad.

I wish people would understand that low-tech solutions
can have great impact. The person reading the MedicAlert®
bracelet or necklace does not need anything more than the
ability to read. Our system is simple, but it works.

Program Staffing

The CaringKind Wanderer's Safety Program has only two employees other than Elizabeth. This program is inexpensive for CaringKind to operate, but it has meaningful impact.

Dementia-friendly clinical settings can also have meaningful impact. When the care systems and clinical settings are designed with the cognitive challenges of someone living with dementia in mind, they can help mitigate adverse physical and emotional events.

Every time you change the place or the people who are interacting with the person with dementia, disorientation and fear increases. We need standardized models of care that address changing caregivers and locations for dementia patients. (Davina Porock)

DAVINA POROCK, PHD

At the time of her interview, Davina Porock was the Vice Provost for Faculty and Administration at Lehman College, City University of New York. She has practiced nursing and conducted dementia research nationally and internationally.

In her interview, Davina highlighted the importance of not moving people with dementia around as much as other patients in the hospital setting. Those with dementia become easily disoriented and frightened when moved into a loud emergency department, then into a new room on another floor, and then around for different tests and procedures. Davina suggested providers should adjust their systems to enable patients with dementia to be in one quiet place as much as possible.

Davina also described how the built environment within a clinical setting can support patients with dementia. People with dementia have visual spatial challenges. Davina gave an example from a long-term care facility in the United Kingdom where she had previously worked. The bathrooms were all white. Patients were unable to find exactly where the toilet was and often ended up sitting in the wrong place, resulting in discomfort or a fall. When they changed the toilet seat to black, this issue was resolved.

Patients with dementia often like to walk around. The management of a long-term care facility that Davina worked for installed pictures at the end of each hallway that changed electronically to keep people occupied and to make the walk more interesting. The management also simplified the signage and made it yellow and black, which is the last color differences that can be seen by someone with dementia. The signs were hung at eye height so people did not have to look up for them.

These methods resulted in lowering the length of stay for people with dementia. Normally a person with dementia, who presents with the same illness or injury of a person without dementia, will stay longer in a care facility. With the dementia-friendly interventions, Davina and her team were able to make those stay times equal.

Dementia-friendly clinical settings are growing in importance as the rates of dementia continue to multiply. They are steps toward building a society that is welcoming and inclusive for those living with dementia. The Dementia Action Alliance[45] is dedicated to building a dementia-inclusive America.

We are trying to respectfully disrupt the beliefs, attitudes, and practices about dementia in our country. (Karen Love)

KAREN LOVE, JACKIE PINKOWITZ, AND LON PINKOWITZ
THE DEMENTIA ACTION ALLIANCE

Karen Love is the Founder and Executive Director, Jackie Pinkowitz is the Chair of the Board, and Lon Pinkowitz serves on the Board of Directors of the Dementia Action Alliance (DAA).

The DAA envisions a society where dementia symptoms are better understood and accommodated as a disability, and individuals and families living with dementia are fully included and supported.

The DAA is a diverse coalition of passionate people, organizations, companies, and communities that are "committed to creating a better society now for individuals to live with dementia." The Alliance enables numerous learning exchanges among diverse stakeholders, including those living with dementia, through:

- The Advisory Council of persons living with dementia symptoms provides guidance from the perspective of their lived experience. Their insight and input are crucial to the vision, mission, and goals of the DAA.

- The Scientific Advisory Board is comprised of professionals with diverse knowledge and expertise about person-centered dementia care and services across research, policy, and practice. The board provides technical, clinical, and scientific guidance for advancing DAA initiatives.

- Workgroups: Optimizing Well-being, Technology, Arts and Dementia.

- An online resources center.

- Community presentations and conversations.

We want healthcare clinicians to understand that
people living with dementia are people first and
patients second. (Jackie Pinkowitz)

Stigma

In their 2016 white paper, "Walk with Me,"[46] the Canadian Research
Institute for Aging[47] identified three barriers that prevent older adults
from living life fully. Those barriers include ageism and stigma,
segregation from community, and the pervasive medicalized and
deficit-focused views on aging. People with dementia often feel a sense
of shame and reduced status within society.[48] Many seek to hide their
diagnosis.[49] Some resort to isolating themselves from their community.
Caregivers and families feel the stigma by association, adding stress to
an already overwhelming care burden.[50] Stigmas focus on limitations
rather than strengths. This is juxtaposed to how people with dementia
wish to be viewed.[51] The DAA hopes to reduce the stigma of dementia
through connection and conversation.

It is all too easy to see someone's challenges
before we see the person. (Karen Love)

Caring Conversations are friendly, informal gatherings aimed at
changing the perceptions of people living with dementia. The DAA hosts
conversations in communities throughout the US. The conversations
always include people living with dementia and are open to the community, including healthcare professionals, local law enforcement, business

owners, and caregivers. Karen, Jackie, and Lon view the conversations as small, community, dementia-related think tanks. The community members can interact with people who are living with dementia and learn about them as people, which help participants see the person before their disease. Karen mentioned that it is their hope that when participants leave the conversation, they will say, "There is the artist," rather than, "There is the woman with dementia." Jackie hopes that these conversations will build community champions who will carry the conversations further and promote dementia inclusion in their community.

The DAA strives to dispel the myth that those living with dementia are not vital contributors to their communities and to society as a whole. In their interview, Karen, Jackie, and Lon expressed the importance of involving the stakeholders in all areas of policy that affect those living with dementia. In this case, stakeholders might include caregivers, families, and more obviously people living with dementia. Karen expressed her disappointment that the US government built a federal advisory council for dementia that included researchers and clinicians, but no people living with dementia. Jackie used the phrase "Nothing about us without us," which was the title of an influential book about disability.[52] Karen, Jackie, and Lon believe that communities and businesses should adapt to include people living with dementia as they have for those living with disability. Some from the DAA Advisory Board have brought their perspectives to local, state, and federal policy makers and remain active in the world of dementia policy. One of those advisors is Brian LeBlanc.

Hopefully we can inspire honest conversations and slowly chip away at the pervasive stigma and fear that surround dementia. (Brian LeBlanc)

BRIAN LEBLANC
DEMENTIA ACTION ALLIANCE

Brian LeBlanc is a public speaker and dementia advocate. He is the fourth generation in his family to have Alzheimer's disease. He is on the advisory board of the DAA and the leadership board of Covenant Care. He is also on the National Early Stage advisory group of the Alzheimer's Association.

Brian speaks publicly and advocates tirelessly so people can understand that those living with Alzheimer's disease are "people like everyone else" who offer value to society. He shares his personal history and journey with the disease because too many hide their diagnosis for fear of being treated differently. He mentioned in his interview that he does not try to "paint a rosy picture" of Alzheimer's disease because it is difficult, but he wants the public to see him as a man who likes to go to concerts and Disneyland before they see his struggles.

Brian is a musician and he loves to sing. He described how the faces of the residents in memory care light up when he performs for them. He had some friends ask him whether it made him uncomfortable to see people in the later stages of dementia. He responded, "I hope someone like me will come and sing songs to me when I am in their position."

Brian mentioned that he has good days and bad days. Recently he lost his ability to speak. This was a stressful period for him and his family. After a couple of weeks, and during an anniversary trip with his wife Shannon to Disneyland, Brian's ability to speak returned. When he described this he said, "Disneyland is the happiest place on earth." In one of his blogs, Brian wrote that he has not stopped talking since, and when his family is away he talks to his dog Dallas, who is a great listener and never disagrees. In his blog, *Alzheimer's: The Journey*, Brian shares his experience of living with Alzheimer's.[53] He can also be found advocating on Facebook, LinkedIn, and Twitter. The tagline of his blog reads, "I have Alzheimer's BUT, it doesn't have me!" We believe him.

Our next chapter describes the way forward to sustainably care for the global aging population by merging health and social supports to address the biopsychosocial and environmental needs of older adults. This upstream facing idea aims to meet needs that, if unmet, result in physical and mental illness and injury. It carries with it more than an ounce of prevention and improves patient engagement resulting in greatly reduced healthcare utilization and spending.

The full interviews referenced in this chapter can be found at this link: www.accessh.org/agingwell.

9

Merging Health and Social Services

Merging health and social care, including prevention, to improve quality of life and well-being is a form of population health that is especially effective for the older population. In 1993, the seminal article by McGinnis and Foege shined light on the fact that the United States needs to integrate more social supports and prevention into the healthcare system.[1] The article claimed that 95 percent of healthcare spending in the US goes to medical care, while only 5 percent is dedicated to population health measures. McGinnis and Foege make the case that the imbalance of health to social care expenditure is the reason for the poor health outcomes realized in the US. The authors attributed 40 percent of deaths to behaviors, 30 percent to genetics, 15 percent to social determinants, and 5 percent to environmental exposures. This left 10 percent of health outcomes attributable to medical care. In the following years, the quote has been repeated over and over, and the percentage of health outcomes attributable to health care has been adapted over time. The highest percentage quoted is 30. Most experts use the quote that is considered generous: Health care is only responsible for 20 percent of health outcomes.

Health is a state of complete physical, mental, and social well-being and not merely the absence of disease or infirmity.[2] (World Health Organization)

Today people are living with increasing health and social needs over a longer period of time. In response, best practices in aging shift the main goal of care from curing illness to improving the quality of life and well-being in the extra years people live. This goal is often referred to as shortening the gap between life expectancy and healthy life expectancy.[3]

Public and private health systems that serve older adults are steadily moving toward comprehensive approaches that integrate health care with social supports and prevention. This approach includes non-clinical, individualized interventions that support the biological, psychological, social, and environmental needs and honor the priorities of the patient. The approach also maintains a focus on the social determinants of health of the patient.

The fact that medical care historically has had limited impact on the health of populations has been known for many years.[4]

The interviews summarized below detail interventions that address the social determinants of health, including the condition, accessibility, and safety of the home; community connection and inclusion;[5] and access to health care, transportation, and food. The interviewees also describe preventative programs for chronic disease self-management, medication management and review, improving function, increasing independence, and mitigating the risk of falling.

The Home Environment

Staying at home is cost-effective and keeps people connected to their community supports and activities. The home environment can also present risk factors that need to be mitigated to preserve function, independence, health, safety, and quality of life.

Access to Care

Access to care is an ongoing problem for older adults who have challenges leaving and returning home. These challenges are often due to the lack of adequate transportation and the need for home modifications such as wider doorways, more supportive railings, and elevators, or ramps. Bringing care and support to the home and community can improve access for this cohort.

Access to Transportation

Lack of transportation is a barrier to successful aging in place. In 2015, an estimated 54 percent, totaling 3.9 million older adults, faced challenges accessing transportation.[6] In the same year, an estimated 15.5 million older adults lived in communities with poor or no public transportation.[7] Older adults without access to transportation are more likely to remain isolated at home, miss visits to the doctor, and not make necessary errands, including shopping for groceries, resulting in further physical and mental health decline.

Access to Food

Food insecurity as defined by the US Department of Agriculture is a lack of consistent access to enough food for an active healthy life.[8] In 2015, more than eight percent of older adults in the United States experienced food insecurity.[9] That percent is projected to double by 2025.[10] Food insecurity has negative health and well-being implications. Older adults who are food insecure experience similar levels of inability to perform the activities of daily living[11] as seniors who are 14 years older but are food secure.[12] Food insecure seniors are more likely to be depressed and in poor or fair health.[13]

Malnutrition[14] can be caused by many factors including, the inability to afford groceries or leave the house and travel to a grocery store, medications that cause stomach upset, and dental problems, including ill-fitting dentures and tooth decay. Malnutrition in older adults leads to falls,[15] physical and cognitive decline, and mortality.[16] Sixty percent of seniors who present at the emergency department arrive at risk for malnutrition or already malnourished.[17]

Chronic Disease Self-Management

Approximately 80 percent of seniors have at least one chronic disease and 68 percent have two or more.[18] Chronic disease self-management empowers older adults with knowledge and planning to keep their chronic illnesses in check and to manage the associated conditions. Validated programs have shown to improve quality of life and lower health system usage and cost[19] by significantly reducing emergency department visits and hospitalizations.[20] On average, the number of chronic illnesses that people live with increases with age.[21] As the number of chronic illnesses a person has increases, so does the likeliness of poor functional status,[22] resulting in declining ability to perform the activities of daily living.[23]

Medication Management

Almost half of all prescriptions in the US are for older adults.[24] The more medications one takes, the higher the risk of adverse drug reactions.[25,26,27] Older adults are at a higher risk for adverse drug reactions.[28] Ten to 30 percent of hospital admissions of older adults are attributed to adverse drug reactions.[29] That number rises to 33 percent for people older than 75.[30] Adverse drug reactions result in high healthcare usage and costs and cause substantial morbidity and mortality.[31] An estimated 40 to 50 percent of seniors who are aging in place and receiving home or community-based care are not taking their medications properly.[32] Approximately one half of adverse drug reactions in older adults are preventable.[33]

Function and Independence

Independence, aging in place, and quality of life are heavily dependent on the ability to perform the activities of daily living (ADLs). Having the ability to perform the ADLs is the number one factor of quality of life for those living with dementia.[34] Limitations in performing ADLs are predictors for early nursing home admission, frailty, and mortality.[35]

Older adult falls are increasing and, sadly, often herald the
end of independence. Healthcare providers can make fall
prevention a routine part of care in their practice, and older
adults can take steps to protect themselves.[36] (Tom Frieden,
MD, MPH, former Director of the CDC)

Falls

The World Health Organization considers falls to be a major global
public health crisis.[37] Falls are the leading cause of death and injury for
older adults.[38] Globally, the more than 37 million falls that are severe
enough to require medical attention are responsible for more than 17
million disability adjusted life years[39] lost.[40] Falls can also result in costly
nursing home admissions.[41] In the US, one in four people age 65 and
older falls annually, sending an older adult to the emergency department
every 11 seconds.[42] After a fall, a person is twice as likely to fall again.[43]
The average cost of hospitalization for a fall of an older adult is more
than US$30,000, and 800,000 older adults are hospitalized annually as
a result of a fall.[44] The annual medical costs of falls of older adults in the
US are estimated at US$31 billion.[45] The benefit for home modification
interventions to prevent falls for older adults has shown to be at least 12
times the cost of the intervention.[46] That benefit increases by 60 percent
for those who have already experienced a fall.[47]

The American health system does not invest in social services
and prevention the way it should. Partners in Care is trying to
impact that allocation. (June Simmons)

JUNE SIMMONS

PARTNERS IN CARE FOUNDATION[48]

June Simmons is the founder of the Partners in Care Foundation and a co-founder of the national Evidence-Based Leadership Council.[49] Partners in Care collaborates with providers to pilot interventions for prevention and chronic disease self-management. After the proof-of-concept phase of the interventions, Partners in Care encourages health system uptake, with the goal of making the evidence-based programs standard protocol.

> Any payer is happy with cost savings
> and better health outcomes.

Readmissions

In her interview, June noted that more than 15 percent[50] of patients insured through Medicare are readmitted to the hospital within one month of discharge, costing Medicare US$26 billion annually[51]—US$17 billion of that is deemed preventable. The Partners in Care Transition Choices[52] program is designed to prevent readmissions by engaging home and community care networks to provide follow-up care and social supports such as transportation and food. Additionally, they conduct risk assessments to prevent medication conflicts and falls. The care team also provides chronic disease self-management coaching.

Nursing Home Avoidance

Nursing homes have become the default, post-discharge route because Medicare reimburses for up to 100 days of nursing home stay after hospital discharge. Without safe, coordinated, multidisciplinary care available in the home, many patients have no option other than nursing homes (skilled nursing facilities) for recuperative care upon hospital discharge. Because nursing homes also offer permanent "custodial" care, it can be easy to become "stuck" there and never make it back home. Nursing homes are not the best option for many post-hospital patients, and they also have high rates of readmission. The Partners in Care transitions program enables hospitals to discharge patients directly to their homes.[53] The program results in improved customer satisfaction and cost savings. The net savings to Medicare from 30,000 people who participated in the care transitions program are estimated at US$21 million.

> One of the biggest issues in health care is the lack of coordination. This lack of coordination greatly affects medications management.

Medication Review

The goal of the Partners in Care medication review programs is to reduce adverse drug reactions. June mentioned that, according to the Centers for Disease Control, those 65 and older are at twice the risk of going to the emergency department due to adverse drug reactions, compared with all those under age 65. Older adults are also 7 times more likely to be admitted to the hospital from the emergency department than other cohorts. June also noted that nearly 177,000 seniors experience emergency department visits and 100,000 are admitted to the hospital each year due to adverse drug reactions. The HomeMeds and HomeMedsPlus medication safety programs target older, frail people living with multiple chronic conditions who have recently been discharged from the hospital or nursing home. This cohort takes many medications and is at a high risk of complications. They are also often under the care of multiple specialists who might not be coordinating the medications they are prescribing. Hospitalizations generally result in the doctor prescribing more medications that have potential conflict with others the patient has at home. The prescriptions might be duplications with a different name, color, or shape than medications the patient is already taking and will continue to take after discharge.

Partners in Care designed software to support their medication review. The medication library is updated regularly because medications change often. The evidence-based algorithms detect certain medication conflicts, potential adverse effects like risk for gastrointestinal bleeding, falls, dizziness or confusion, and duplications. Any potential medication-related problems are reviewed by a pharmacist who then makes recommendations for any needed changes to the patient's primary care physician. Partners in Care provides online training and periodic reviews with organizations that implement HomeMeds as part of their care plan. To date, the HomeMeds and HomeMedsPlus programs are operational at 73 sites in 20 states.

Certain classes of drugs, such as psychotropics, cardiovascular medications, and non-steroidal anti-inflammatory drugs, are especially dangerous and problematic when used improperly.

During her interview, June shared some stories from the medication review field. One older gentleman who started falling when he returned home from the hospital was dedicated to taking all his medications. Unfortunately, he was taking them all at once at breakfast so he would not forget any. The falls were occurring because he was taking multiple doses of blood pressure medication at the same time and one of his medications was a sleeping pill. Another patient wanted to be sure to follow the instructions to take her medications with food. The directions on the medications were to take them three times per day. Because the patient only ate one meal per day at lunchtime, she was taking all of her medications at one time.

The HomeMeds program is a medication safety review. The HomeMedsPlus program includes psychosocial, functional, fall-risk, and environmental assessments with the medication review. A care manager uses the information gleaned from the assessments and review to design individualized care and service plans. The assessments are a form of upstream prevention that address the social determinants of health such as a hole in the roof or lack of food, transportation, or temperature control.

Although the assessments and the services delivered can be relatively simple, they have profound impact (Fig. 9.1). A recent pilot program resulted in a 22 percent lower rate of hospital readmissions and a nearly 13 percent lower rate of emergency department visits. The estimated cost savings from hospital avoidance was 53 percent. In addition, 77 percent of the patients needed equipment or home modifications to improve their ability to live safely at home. The medication reviews revealed medication problems for 63 percent of the patients visited. Fifty-four percent of the patients visited had psychosocial risk factors, including depression, issues with caregiving, and financial concerns. June noted that the outcomes might seem surprising because the patients visited were receiving high-quality medical care, but this highlights the importance of addressing non-medical issues to avoid hospital readmissions. June also mentioned that she was encouraged by the fact that 84 percent of the patients who were offered HomeMedsPlus accepted and completed the program.

Partners in Care uses clinicians who are already visiting the home to conduct the assessments and medication reviews. This saves on time and transportation costs. Non-clinicians can also conduct the review. June suggested that possibly volunteers or meal delivery people could be enlisted to conduct the reviews to keep the costs low and improve access.

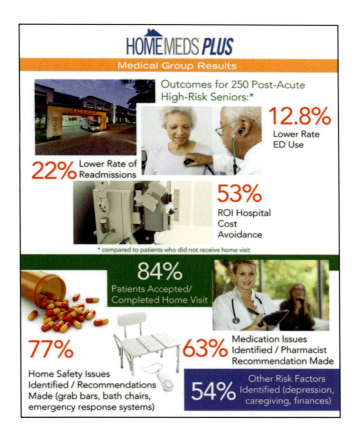

Figure 9.1 Results of HomeMeds Plus pilot program. Source: Partners in Care Foundation

Many are working to escalate the needed changes in
population health management to make the disruptive home
and community-based interventions readily available.

Chronic Disease Self-Management and Education

Kaiser Permanente and Stanford University collaborated to design
chronic disease self-management education programs. Insurers offer
the program to their patients to improve health outcomes. Partners in
Care provides the programs within a seven-miles radius of clusters of
patients because they found that transportation was a barrier to patient
participation. The programs are also available online along with a self-
study toolkit. Because the evidence-based programs have resulted in cost
reduction through improved chronic disease management, governmental
entities are interested in expanding them throughout the US.

Why would you address falls without conducting a
medication review? Why address chronic disease without
diabetes, or diabetes without hypertension? These
programs are meant to work together.

PREVENTION

Partners in Care collaborated with leaders around the US to create the
Evidence-Based Leadership Council that collaboratively designs and
disseminates evidence-based preventative programs for balance and falls,

fitness, exercise, and chronic disease self-management. The programs include: A Matter of Balance,[54] Healthy IDEAS,[55] PEARLS,[56] Healthy Moves,[57] EnhanceWellness,[58] EnhanceFitness,[59] and Fit and Strong.[60] Community organizations offer the programs at the local level across the country.

Another program that blends healthcare delivery with social support is CAPABLE (Community Aging in Place—Advancing Better Living for Elders).

> As a nurse making house calls in Baltimore, I have seen patients who had to crawl to the front door to let me in. Others had to throw me the keys from the upper window because they could not come down to the first floor to open the door.[61] (Sarah Szanton)

SARAH SZANTON
CAPABLE[62]

Sarah Szanton is the Director of Policy for the Center on Innovative Care in Aging[63] and Professor at the Johns Hopkins School of Nursing. She studies health disparities in older adults and works to eliminate health and quality-of-life differences for seniors across socioeconomic and racial lines.

House calls are not the same as treating someone in an
office setting. I came face to face with what mattered to
people when I was in their home. I saw a clear picture of the
environment they were living in. I found holes in floors
and shaky bannisters.

The CAPABLE program engages a home repair professional, an occupational therapist, and a nurse over a four-month period to support the functional goals and medical priorities of older people who wish to remain living at home. CAPABLE participants are mostly low-income, African American people age 65 and older and have limitations with one or more ADL and two or more independent activities of daily living (IADLs).[64] The aim of the program is to improve physical function as measured by the ability to perform the ADLs and IADLs. This type of program is referred to as restorative care in many countries because the focus is on functional improvement. Goal-oriented programs empower patients to direct their own care and support through varied, and often competing, health and social needs. The success of goal-oriented care is measured, in part, by the ability to meet the goals of the patient.

My patient was the same person. She had lived the same
101 years. She had the same physiology and biology,
yet she needed less medication because
of the physical environment.

Honoring the Goals of the Participant

The CAPABLE team members meet individually with the program participant, and the occupational therapist designs a work order based on the participant's goals. In her interview, Sarah noted that the success of the program is dependent upon the team honoring the goals of the participant over what the team members think the goals should be. Sarah believes that the program is successful because participants are engaged and determined when they are challenged to meet their own goals. Participant goals might include being able to go downstairs or upstairs in their home, prepare meals, or take a shower. To support the goal of someone who wants to go up and down the stairs, the home repair team member will likely install a second bannister, make the existing bannister more secure, and add brighter lighting to the staircase. The occupational therapist might work on arm and leg strength. For the participant who wishes to prepare meals, the home repairs professional might widen the doorway for wheelchair access to the kitchen, adjust counter tops, and install a refrigerator and stove that are accessible to someone in a wheelchair. For the participant wishing to shower, the occupational therapist might work on balance and strength while the home repair team member would install grab bars in the shower and around bathroom. For most concerns the nurse would conduct a medication review to ensure that functional issues are not a result of medication duplication or error.

We created a new role for nurses. Nurses have traditionally not been focused on function to the degree that CAPABLE does.

Outcomes

FUNCTIONAL IMPROVEMENT

Sarah mentioned that she was initially surprised with the outcomes of a recent randomized control trial because no other program has realized nearly the success in functional improvement as CAPABLE. During the Centers for Medicare and Medicaid Innovation project, CAPABLE reduced participant disability by one half. Seventy-five percent of the participants improved their ability to perform the ADLs. The average ADL limitation reduction went from four to two. The CAPABLE team labeled improvements as unsuccessful even if a participant went from no ability to perform an ADL to having only minor limitations performing the same ADL by the end of the program. Sarah noted that this indicates that the results, as positive as they are, are conservative. The IADL improvements realized were also impressive. Sixty-five percent of the participants improved their ability to perform their IADLs. Sarah put these results into further perspective by explaining that this patient population, when not participating in CAPABLE, is likely to experience further functional loss during the four-month period.

Another important outcome of improved function is that improved ability to perform the ADLs and IADLs prevents falls. This is why CAPABLE was recently named a leading falls prevention program by the National Council on Aging.

QUALITY OF LIFE AND MENTAL HEALTH

Participants who are able to live in their homes safely and have the functional ability to remain independent experience improved quality of life and less depression. On average, the CAPABLE program participants experienced reduced levels of depression from moderate to mild. This improvement in mental health is not minor. The difference between moderate and mild depression could mean the difference in the need for anti-depressant medication. The improved quality of life of the participants does not end with them. Their well-being affects their families and their communities. Sarah mentioned that many of the CAPABLE participants were foster parents. She also acknowledged the benefit of keeping civically minded, caring older adults functional enough to provide stable parenting for local foster children. It is a win-win for the older adult and the community. Being a foster parent also fulfills the need for purpose and generativity felt by older adults.[65]

HOSPITALIZATIONS AND NURSING HOME PLACEMENTS

CAPABLE participants experienced much lower rates of hospitalization than the control group. They also entered nursing homes at a rate three percent lower than the control group, reducing their likelihood of nursing home placement by 50 percent.

COST

The CAPABLE program generates health system cost savings that are six times the cost of implementation. Because of this savings, providers who receive value-based insurance reimbursements are eager to adopt the program.

Looking Forward

As health systems around the world reorganize to meet the needs of the growing older population, it is our hope at ACCESS Health International that all systems of care for older adults will be designed to treat the whole person, including the biopsychosocial and environmental factors of health. We also envision increasing efforts upstream with improved preventative interventions and a firm eye on the social determinants that drive health system usage, inequity, and suffering. The literature and the two previous interviews provide evidence to support that such a design will improve access to care and support, reduce health system costs, and contribute to well-being.

Social inclusion is crucial to the well-being of older adults. Creating inclusive spaces and communities fills many psychological and social needs of older adults and has shown to improve physical health. Such spaces and communities are a powerful antidote to the pervasive systemic ageist stereotypes and prejudices seen around the world. In our next chapter, we write about inspiring programs that connect older adults to their communities and enable a life of purpose, inclusion, learning, and intergenerational connections.

The full interviews referenced in this chapter can be found at this link: www.accessh.org/agingwell.

10

Purpose and Social Inclusion

Social exclusion contributes to loneliness and social isolation. Both have profound psychological and physical implications in older individuals that adversely affect their quality of life.[1,2,3] Loneliness is associated with increased mortality and functional limitation[4,5,6,7,8] and has been linked to increased rates of depression.[9] Loneliness and social isolation are challenges faced by societies around the world.[10,11,12,13]

Social inclusion is a core component of optimal aging. Retirement, the loss of a spouse or friends, children living far away, the inability to drive, and physical or cognitive limitations all increase the risk of loneliness in older adults. Those with chronic illness are sometimes prone to self-isolation to avoid the stigma associated with aging, illness, and dementia.[14] Public spaces that are not welcoming and accessible to those who are older, ill, or have cognitive limitations contribute to social isolation. In advanced age, people seek meaning and purpose. They often wish to leave a legacy to the generations that follow their own. Intergenerational connections can fill this need and foster community connection and inclusion. Intergenerational connections are beneficial for society as a whole because they challenge ageist beliefs.[15,16] Such connections also offer older adults the opportunity to fulfill their need for purpose and generativity.[17] Having a purpose contributes to psychological and physical well-being.[18,19,20] Another trend that often leads to intergenerational connections, social inclusion, and purpose is lifelong learning.

> The profound effects of loneliness on health and independence are a critical public health problem. It is no longer medically or ethically acceptable to ignore older adults who feel lonely and marginalized.[21] (Dr. Carla M. Perissinotto, MD, MHS geriatrician, University of California, San Francisco)

Lifelong Learning

Increased lifespans have led to many more years of retirement. Those added retirement years are perfect opportunities for adult education, a trend that is taking place around the world. Some governments are recognizing the need for adult learning and training to support a shrinking workforce.[22] The population of working-age people in China is projected to decline by one third by 2050.[23] Today, China has 60,000 universities for older adults with 7 million students enrolled. The country plans to expand universities for older adults to include one in every city.[24] The Chinese government believes that the universities keep older adults socially engaged, out of old-age homes, and potentially active in the workforce.[25]

> The universities for seniors are in higher demand now because many newly retired are better educated. They are not satisfied with just playing mahjong or gossiping with their friends.[26] (Xiong Fangjie, Vice President of Shanghai University for the Elderly)

Lifelong learning offers older adults the opportunity to learn new information and build a new career, improve health management, enjoy creative studies, or explore other subjects they have always been interested in but did not have the time to pursue until their retirement years. Demand has driven many of the accredited, degree-granting colleges in the United States to offer greatly reduced or free tuition to those 65 and older.[27] Lifelong learning has shown to contribute to general well-being, life satisfaction, and intellectual, social, physical, emotional, and occupational wellness.[28,29]

United Nations Principles for Older Persons

In 1991, the United Nations issued the Principles for Older Persons that encouraged governments of member states to integrate five principles into their policies and programs.[30] All of the principles support social inclusion and optimal aging. The summarized principles are that older people should have:

- Independence, including the ability to age in place, employment opportunities, access to educational programs, and safe and supportive environments that are adapted to their capacities;
- Participation, including active participation in society and the ability to fulfill their need for generativity;[31]

- Care, including the benefit of family and community support, and to be involved in their own care planning;
- Self-fulfillment, including access to education, culture, recreation, and spiritual resources;
- Dignity, including being treated with respect and being valued by society.

This chapter describes housing and community models and interventions that support the principles outlined by the United Nations.

Housing

Housing and community are important factors that can help to keep older adults socially and civically engaged. As governments seek sustainable housing options for their older residents, the focus is often on enabling aging in place because living at home is far less expensive than living in independent or assisted living communities. Two community models developed organically in the US. Driven by residents who had aged together and wished to stay in their homes and connected to their community, these models integrate health care and social services with housing and community. They also have a strong social component.

> We wanted to be active and taking care of ourselves
> and each other rather than being taken care of.
> (Beacon Hill Village)[32]

The Village Movement

The Village Movement began in 2002 in Beacon Hill, Boston.[33] The Village concept was born out of residents' desire to remain connected to their community as they aged. Villages are member-run, self-supporting grassroots organizations. The Village hires staff to oversee the collective delivery of health, social, and other services that make it possible for the members to remain in their community. Many Village members, who are independent and still working, join their local Village for the robust social activities that are individualized to the community.

Because of their size, the Village community has leveraging power on prices. Members receive discounts including:

- Gym membership, classes, and trainers;
- Drivers (rides to doctor-prescribed visits are free);
- Computer help offered free of charge by volunteers or for a discounted rate by professionals;
- Handyman;
- Home health assistance;
- Companions;
- Cooking classes;
- Social programs.

The Village members engage in community activities and social events including:

- Cultural arts excursions;
- Talks by local experts about cultural, political, health and wellness, and memory topics;
- Lunches, coffees, cocktail parties, and special interest groups;
- Day trips to local attractions.[34]

Villages are financially accessible to many because fees are considerably less expensive than moving to independent and assisted living communities. The national average for a private one bedroom in assisted living is US$3,628 per month.[35] A one bedroom in independent living varies from state to state, ranging from US$1,399 in South Dakota to US$4,002 in Massachusetts.[36] A Beacon Hill Village monthly membership costs US$675 for an individual and US$976 for a household. Discounted monthly memberships are available to lower- and moderate-income individuals who are 60 and older. Those monthly fees range from US$110 for an individual to US$160 for a household. Members who join only for the social activities pay approximately US$250 per month for a household.[37]

The Beacon Hill Village has approximately 400 members who are 50 and over who live in Beacon Hill, Back Bay, North End, South End, and surrounding neighborhoods. The Beacon Hill Village members were inspired to create the Village to Village Network to exchange ideas and new tools with the other villages around the country and the world.[38] Villages promote active, productive community engagement and autonomy for the residents. A slightly different housing model that promotes the same community qualities is the naturally occurring retirement community.

Naturally Occurring Retirement Communities

The first naturally occurring retirement community (NORC) began in 1986 in New York City. NORCs vary. They can be situated in subsidized housing complexes, neighborhoods with private homes, condominiums and cooperatives, and rental apartment buildings. In these communities, most residents moved in at a younger age, raised their children, and continued to stay in their homes and age together. Specifications for NORCs have continued to change over time, but approximately 40 percent or more of the residents in NORCs are over 60.

With governmental and philanthropic funding, public and private community-based organizations collaborate in the NORC Supportive Service Program (NORC-SSP) to deliver services to the community members, including health care, health promotion and prevention, psychological support, social and educational activities, and social services, including meals. This proactive population health service delivery is possible because the older adults reside in concentrated locations. NORC residents actively participate in needs assessments and program planning with building owners, housing managers, local businesses, local law enforcement, and civic, religious, and cultural institutions to shape an inclusive community that enables them to live in their homes as they age. The number of NORCs has risen along with the growth in the aging population. As of 2012 there were 315 NORCs in the world and 50,000 older adults living in more than 40 NORCs in New York alone.[39]

JDC-ESHEL

JDC-ESHEL is a model similar to the NORC-SSP that has existed in Israel for the past 45 years. The US-based non-governmental organization, the Joint Distribution Committee (JDC), and the Association for the Planning and Development of Services for the Aged in Israel (ESHEL) coordinate with public and private entities to deliver services to older community residents. The model gives seniors the option to remain living at home and connected to their social circle rather than move into expensive institutional residences. Some have claimed that JDC-ESHEL provides a "multiplier effect throughout the entire health and social services sectors."[40]

Another housing model that is based in the culture of social engagement, intergenerational connections, and community and civic engagement is cohousing.

Cohousing

Israel has a 100-year-old country-specific version of cohousing called kibbutzim. Kibbutz are home to 120,000 Israelis.[41] The cohousing model we will describe, Bofaellesskaber, began with the community, Skråplanet in Denmark in 1964, inspired by the publication of "The Missing Link Between Utopia and the Dated One-Family House," by architect Jan Gudmand-Hoyer. The model eventually spread to countries around the world. Today there are approximately 700 cohousing communities in Denmark. In the US, there are 165 established cohousing communities and another 304 in varying stages of completion and occupancy.[42]

Cohousing communities are often referred to as intentional collaborative neighborhoods. The communities are founded on mutual support between the residents who wish to live in close contact with their neighbors and share occasional meals, enjoy common spaces, participate in common activities, and help each other when a need arises. Cohousing communities are naturally multigenerational with the exception of senior-only cohousing communities.

Common characteristics of a cohousing community include:

- Decisions are made by a consensus of community members;
- Communities contain a balance of private homes and community spaces;
- Structures are designed to promote interaction and connection;
- Residents care for each other.

A central design element of cohousing communities is the common house that contains a kitchen, dining room/event space, and other public spaces such as a laundry room, guest room, gym, and play room for children. Residents use the common kitchen to cook meals that are shared with the cohousing community at varying intervals, depending on the community. Cooking responsibilities rotate and the residents each contribute to the cost of the shared meals.

Cohousing community structures are designed so that residents will connect with each other. In the private homes, it is common to have a window above the kitchen sink that faces outdoor areas where neighbors pass by. Parking spaces are separate from the housing areas, so when people park, they naturally walk through the community.

In 2012, cohousing residents reported positive outcomes of living in intentional neighborhoods including:

- 96% had increased satisfaction with life as a result of living in cohousing;
- 75% felt that they were experiencing better health than others in their age group;
- 96% had voted in the last presidential election.[43]

> The overarching characteristic of cohousing is that we know our neighbors well. (Joani Blank)

JOANI BLANK
COHOUSING ENTHUSIAST AND RESIDENT

Joani Blank has lived in cohousing since 1991. At the time of the interview, she was 78 years old and lived in the Swan's Market Cohousing community in Oakland, California. Since our meeting, Joani passed away to the disappointment of the community that embraced her. Her daughter, son in law, and their newborn baby now live in Joani's former home and are bringing three new young residents to the Swan's Market community.

It is common for future residents to participate in designing new cohousing communities. This process is called participatory or cooperative design.[44] Joani explained that the first 11 residents of the Swan's Market cohousing community participated in the design and planning of the structure over a five-year period. The cohousing community sits within a larger commercial space that includes restaurants, shops, art galleries, and apartments.[45] The residents also have convenient access to other amenities in the bustling city of Oakland, California.

Joani Blank in front of the Swan's Market Cohousing community garden

Joani explained that cohousing communities have some common features, but each community is personalized to the residents. One community that Joani visited had a library in the common house because two retired librarians lived in the community. The library was used regularly by residents of all ages, and the librarians took pleasure in managing and promoting it.

The ideology of cohousing is really about creating neighborhood in a new way.

Joani shared her feelings that regular social engagement with her neighbors is possible without compromising the need for privacy. She mentioned that as America has grown, communities have become spread out with large lawns and fences separating one home from the other. Even in urban areas with multifamily buildings, often the residents do not form supportive relationships with each other.

Shared Meals

The residents in cohousing partake in shared meals. In Swan's Market cohousing, they share three common meals each week. Two residents prepare the meals together. Meal preparation is generally looked upon as a fun opportunity to try new recipes. With that schedule, each resident is required to make dinner only once every four and a half weeks. This is convenient for everyone, but especially so for older people who may not want the burden of dinner preparation and do not wish to dine alone. The average cost to enjoy a prepared meal at Swan's Market cohousing is US$4.75.

When anything needs doing, we do it together. That is the way you do things in a community.

Shared Decisions and Projects

Cohousing residents make decisions about the operation and maintenance of the community collectively. The residents of the Swan's Market formed committees, including finance, garden, group process, common house, maintenance, external relations, technology, and social. The committees also oversee the group workdays and special building and grounds maintenance projects.

INTERGENERATIONAL CONNECTIONS

At the time of our interview, the Swan's Market cohousing community was home to 28 adults; one college student, one teenager, and a toddler. Joani shared that the multigenerational nature of cohousing is beneficial for all the residents. Parents, especially single parents, receive much support from the other residents. Children who have grandparents living far away live next door to older people who have the time and interest in forming grandparent-type relationships. Joani's grandchildren are older and live far away. It makes her happy to care for the toddler who lives three doors away. The younger people are willing to go up on a ladder for older residents who are no longer comfortable with that and other tasks. Joani also mentioned that the younger generations are willing and able to help their fellow older residents with technology.

Independent and assisted living residences also have the ability to build intergenerational connections, inclusive communities, and lifelong learning. We described the models of person-centered long-term care of St. Johns and Beatitudes previously in Chap. 2. Here, we wish to highlight their programs that create purposeful connections between residents and the local community.

REBECCA PRIEST
ST. JOHN'S HOME

Rebecca Priest is the Administrator of Skilled Nursing at St. John's Home. Rochester, New York-based St. John's is a full-spectrum senior services provider with four home and village-like campuses.

St. John's long-term care has a privately operated day care on campus and the children visit the residents daily. They also engage in programs with the residents such as building snowmen in the courtyard in winter and participating in planting events in the spring.[46]

St. John's has a long-standing practice of residents participating in intergenerational courses at the St. John Fisher College. In autumn of 2016, a group of ten residents from St. John's Meadows and Brickstone by St. John's joined in the "Campaigns and Elections" class discussion several times throughout the semester. According to professor, Dr. Kathleen Donovan, having residents join the class led to a more informed conversation on politics. "For many students, this was the first election they have paid any attention to, so they have no reference point. Having citizens who have experienced elections as an adult is incredibly helpful."

St. John's Collaborative for Intergenerational Learning is an educational program for Nazareth College students and residents from St. John's. At the beginning of each semester, a group of residents from St. John's Meadows and Brickstone by St. John's join a class of Nazareth students to describe the aging process from their perspective. Many of the Nazareth College students are studying to become physical, occupational, and speech therapists. The collaborative helps future clinicians understand the patients they will be interacting with throughout their careers.

St. John's Home gift shop volunteer Leah Cocilova visits with resident and fellow volunteer Ann Giglia

St. John's Meadows and Brickstone by St. John's independent living campuses have a continual stream of social activities that are run, established, or inspired by the residents.[47,48] The Brickstone campus has meeting spaces, restaurants, and other businesses that are open to the public. These promote meaningful social connections with the residents' peers and younger community members. Beatitudes Campus is another example of senior living that is continually abuzz with resident activities and events.[49]

Our campus is based on purposeful living. (Tena Alonzo)

TENA ALONZO, KAREN MITCHELL, AND IVAN HILTON
BEATITUDES CAMPUS

Tena Alonzo is the Director of Education and Research and the Director of the Comfort Matters™ program at Beatitudes Campus.[50] Karen Mitchell is an Educator of Comfort Matters.[51] Ivan Hilton is the Director of Business Development for Comfort Matters. Phoenix, Arizona-based Beatitudes Campus is a life plan community (sometimes referred to as a continuing care retirement community) with 700 residents.

Beatitudes Campus partners with local schools for the students to visit the campus as part of their service project requirement. One student is honored monthly, and the campus residents are the competition judges. Some of the Beatitudes campus residents contribute to scholarships for local high school students who are presented at a banquet at the end of the school year. There are many residents who are former teachers and education is still their mission.

> We are a life plan community without walls.

Beatitudes has 97 clubs and meetings that were started by and are run by residents. Many in the baby boomer generation were civically active throughout their lives and are leading clubs at Beatitudes to continue their civic engagement. One group, Seniors for a Sustainable Future, traveled to Washington, DC, to lobby.

Some of the Beatitudes residents feel a dedication to the lesbian, gay, bisexual, and transgender (LGBT) community in Phoenix. They began a LGBT support group for campus residents and the Phoenix community. The group meets weekly and has 150 members.

Beatitudes also hosts activities of many outside organizations that are open to the residents. Community members of all ages can enjoy a meal in the campus restaurants and bars that are open to the public.

Beatitudes hosts a weekly concert called a Hootenanny that is organized by Igor Glen, a resident who is a professional musician. Musicians who are residents play along with local community members and Igor Glen.

Lasell Village is also a hub of intergenerational connections and social activities, but what makes the Village even more unique is that it takes lifelong learning a step further than other life plan, or continuing care, retirement communities.

ANNE DOYLE
LASELL VILLAGE

Anne Doyle is the Vice President of Lasell College and the President of Lasell Village, a life plan community that is on the campus of Lasell College in Newton, Massachusetts.[52]

As the name connotes, Lasell Village is designed like a small village that is comprised of 16 buildings that resemble townhouses. Each building has common areas such as living rooms, courtyards, libraries, classrooms, and meeting rooms. Other amenities include gardens, a swimming pool, a gym, restaurants, a bank, a day care, and a preschool. The demographic profile of the Village resembles that of most life plan communities in the US, with residents ranging from 72 to 103 with an average age of 80.

Lasell Village is home to 225 adults who are committed to lifelong learning. Part of the admissions contract is the requirement for residents to participate in 450 hours of learning annually. At first glance this seems like a rigorous requirement, but Anne Doyle reported that last year the residents averaged 550 hours per resident. Anne estimates that the actual number is higher because, after residents have met the required hours, many discontinue documenting their learning time.

The courses are continually changing and evolving in
response to feedback from the residents and the college. No
idea or suggestion is turned away.

All classes at Lasell College are free to the Village residents. This
presents the opportunity for regular intergenerational contact. The
Intergenerational Educational Program group, including the Associate
Dean of education at the college, a faculty member, a college student,
the head of the Fuss Center for Intergenerational Research and Aging,[53]
Anne Doyle, and two Village staff members plan educational programming based on the feedback and request of the students and residents.
Intergenerational course modules are designed around existing course
content and involve more classroom exchange. In these modules, students, young and old, benefit from insights and ideas shared by different
generations. Occasionally residents teach courses based on the expertise
they have acquired during their lifetimes. Many students from Lasell
College work at the Village and build relationships with the residents
out of the classroom also.

The relationship between residents and traditional college
students often becomes an informal mentor relationship,
which has deep meaning for both.

Anne described the special juxtaposition that exists between the
residents of Lasell Village and the students of Lasell College. The Village residents generally have PhDs, MDs, and a host of other academic
degrees, while 46 percent of the students have parents who have not

completed college. Anne mentioned that the residents take an interest in the success of the students and provide support and encouragement. Some residents help the students with the financial costs of college.

> We are all human beings, no matter our age. We want to stay as engaged as long as we possibly can.

Residents of all physical and cognitive abilities and age are supported in their desire to participate in any classes or activities. Anne noted that, in most life plan communities, the residents living in skilled nursing are segregated from the community, as are those living with cognitive challenges. She mentioned one gentleman who lives in skilled nursing who participates in every rehearsal of the Village chorus, Voices of Experience.[54] The same resident also takes educational courses.

The Village is regularly bustling with intergenerational activity. The preschool and nursery school children can be seen all around the campus as part of their daily activities. They interact with the residents just as children in a village would. On any given day, you can find a resident reading to one of the preschool children in the courtyard or library. You can also hear the children's chorus echoing through the halls. Many of the residents who are retired teachers volunteer at the nursery and preschool and others volunteer at an elementary school just down the street.

Some of the Lasell Village residents continue with their active career lives. Anne collaborates with the State Office of Elder Affairs to create internship positions for residents of the Village who are eager to contribute a stakeholder's perspective.

We have written about examples of residential and institutional housing that is inclusive and supportive of optimal aging. City design and policy that is structured with input by the older residents and that involves multiple sectors can also support optimal aging. Cities that are inclusive to those of all ages and abilities empower people to remain in the workforce if they wish, participate in purposeful activities, and remain respected pillars of their community.

Cities are hubs of creativity, business, social connection, and diversity. They make the culture of a given time and place. It is therefore critical that all are able to participate in the vibrant life of the city. Reconceptualization of key physical and social design features is necessary to gain the full benefit of the contributions older adults bring. (Ruth Finkelstein, former Associate Director of the Robert N. Butler Columbia Aging Center)

Age-Inclusive Cities

Age-inclusive cities, also referred to as age-friendly cities, benefit all generations and strengthen the fabric of society as a whole. The World Health Organization identified eight domains that make a community age-friendly.[55] Those domains are:

1. Outdoor spaces and buildings, including parks, sidewalks, safe streets, outdoor seating, and buildings that are safe and accessible to people of all physical abilities;

2. Transportation, including age-accessible public transportation;

3. Housing, including affordable housing options and homes that are designed or modified so older individuals can age in place;

4. Social participation, including enjoyable activities that are accessible and affordable to the older population;

5. Respect and social inclusion, including intergenerational connections;

6. Civic participation and employment, including volunteer and paid work opportunities;

7. Communication and information, including access to information through a variety of channels because not everyone has a smart phone;

8. Community support and health services, including access to health and social services in the home and community.

In 2014, the Milken Institute Center for the Future of Aging launched the Mayor's Pledge that calls for mayors and other civic leaders to create age-inclusive cities.[56] The institute remains a champion for age-inclusive cities with their annual publication of "Best Cities for Successful Aging" that documents how well cities throughout the US enable their older residents to live safe, purposeful, and healthy lives.[57]

Do not design for me; design with me.

(June M. Fisher, MD,[58] dHealth Summit, 2017)

Stakeholder Involvement

It is vital to involve older adults in planning and designing age-inclusive communities. Far too often, ageism and prejudice lead private organizations, city planners, and policy makers away from soliciting the invaluable insights of the older residents they serve. The AdvantAge

Assessment was designed to ascertain the level of age-friendliness of a community by surveying the community's older residents.

MIA OBERLINK
THE ADVANTAGE INITIATIVE

Mia Oberlink is a senior research associate at the Center for Home Care Policy and Research. She manages the AdvantAge Initiative.[59]

The AdvantAge Initiative survey measures 33 indicators (Appendix) of age-friendliness that fall within four domains, including addressing basic needs, promoting social and civic engagement, optimizing health and well-being, and maximizing independence for the frail and disabled (Fig. 10.1). When a community wishes to become age-inclusive, they contract Mia and her team to distribute the AdvantAge Initiative survey to the residents and develop strategies that address the specific needs revealed by the surveys. The goal of the AdvantAge Initiative is to support the independence of the residents and to empower them to age in place while remaining productive members of the community.

Although there is census and local health department data on older adults available, one of the factors that is often missing is the input, experiences, and perceptions of the residents themselves.

Figure 10.1. AdvantAge Initiative. Age-friendly measures

Mia Oberlink mentioned that the survey regularly reveals common issues, including falls, access to mental health support, access to food, and the desire for more social activities. Each community also presents individualized challenges. Mia and her team engage residents, local community partners, and city government to respond to the challenges. The response might be health or fall prevention interventions, adjusting traffic lights or adding a middle island so older adults can cross streets more safely, organizing meal delivery, and repairing uneven sidewalks. The initiatives that are designed for the specific needs of the neighborhood would not be possible without the input of the older residents.

Another initiative that was born from information solicited directly from older New Yorkers is the Age Smart Employer Initiative. In her former position with Age-Friendly NYC, Ruth Finkelstein conducted community needs assessments in town hall meetings around New York City to listen to the concerns of older residents.

At the end of the town halls, a line of people would form to speak with Ruth. Much to her surprise, most of them wanted help in finding employment. Inspired by this experience, Ruth founded the Age Smart Employer initiative.[60]

RUTH FINKELSTEIN
AGE SMART EMPLOYER AND EXCEEDING
EXPECTATIONS INITIATIVES

Ruth Finkelstein was formerly the Assistant Professor of Health Policy and Management and Associate Director of the Robert N. Butler Columbia Aging Center. Today she is the Executive Director of the Brookdale Center of Healthy Aging at Hunter College and Professor of Urban Public Health.

It is not good for most people to have a 20-year vacation. Financing a 20-year retirement from 40 years of employment simply is not affordable. It is not all about the economics either. People have a need to stay active and engaged in a meaningful life with purpose.

Older Workers

People are living longer, but policy, practice, and culture have not adapted to meet the demand of older workers who need or wish to keep working past the standard retirement age. In her interview, Ruth mentioned that when Social Security became law in the US in 1935, the life expectancy was 61 and the retirement age was 65. Today life expectancy is 83, and the retirement age has remained unchanged. A survey by the Employee Research Institute showed that 90 percent of retirees who obtained paid employment post-retirement did so because they wanted to stay active and involved, and 82 percent reported that they enjoyed working.[61]

Many seniors are not financially prepared for retirement.[62,63] In fact, one in three Americans has nothing saved toward retirement[64] and more than a quarter of the workers 55 and older report having less than US$10,000 in savings and investments.[65] A lack of money to spend as consumers can contribute to isolation.[66] Working an additional year can increase retirement income by 9 percent and working five more years can increase it by 56 percent.[67] Lower-income workers benefit even more from working longer; their retirement realizes a 16 percent increase with one more year of work and a 98 percent increase with an additional five years of work.[68] We should note that the myth that older workers who delay retirement take jobs from younger workers is just that. Due to the size of the baby boom population, the number of those retiring leave more job openings per young person than existed in 1990.[69] This situation exists around the globe and is leading to work-force shortages in many countries.[70] Ruth pointed out that there are 700,000 workers in New York City who are over the age of 50. Many wish to remain in the workforce into their older years.

> Retaining seasoned employees is a matter of good
> economics and good business.

Age Smart Employer is an initiative of the Robert N. Butler Columbia Aging Center that recognizes employers who exemplify best practice in retaining and attracting older employees.[71] Best practice includes: opportunity for phased or part-time retirement, supporting physical limitations, understanding the value of older mentors, presenting opportunities for upward mobility, offering training or continued education, restructuring jobs, and a culture that is steeped in valuing people of all generations. The initiative involves a competition and awards ceremony that garners national attention. Past winners include many small employers that make up the heart of New York City and larger employers, including NYU Langone Medical Center and Brooks Brothers. The awards shine a spotlight on employers who are reaping the benefits of their older workforce.

> Often, aging is treated as a disease, rather than an opportunity to offer society expertise and wisdom in work, volunteerism, civic engagement, and education.

Ageism

Robert Butler classified ageism as a serious form of bigotry that is often overlooked.[72] Ageism is fed by prejudicial stereotyping of older adults that leads to discrimination and stigmatization. It can infiltrate policies and practices of businesses, healthcare providers, city and state planning boards, local culture, and society as a whole. Ageism and negative aging stereotypes contribute to social isolation and segregation, as well as cognitive, psychological, and behavioral decline in older adults.[73]

> What does 80 plus look like today?
> Very much alive and thriving.

Ruth Finkelstein and journalist, Dorian Block, lead the Exceeding Expectations initiative.[74] Exceeding Expectations challenges ageism and the stigma of aging by profiling selected residents of New York City who have lived longer than the average life expectancy of New Yorkers, which is 81. The videos are powerful and touchingly intimate portrayals of vibrant people living active purposeful lives.

City design and policy that support inclusion for those of all ages and abilities challenge aging stereotypes by enabling older residents to remain included and connected to their community. In 2010 New York became the first member of the World Health Organization's Global Network of Age-Friendly Cities.

> Older people are often among the most civically engaged. They add stability and substantial social, intellectual, and financial capital to the community. (Lindsay Goldman)

LINDSAY GOLDMAN
AGE-FRIENDLY NYC[75]

Lindsay Goldman directs the New York Academy of Medicine in its efforts toward healthy aging.

Age-Friendly NYC is a partnership between the Office of the Mayor, the New York City Council, and the New York Academy of Medicine that works to identify and catalyze improvements to enable older people to access, enjoy, and contribute to city life. Age-Friendly NYC asks older New Yorkers about their daily lives and develops strategies to reduce or eliminate barriers to optimal social, physical, and economic participation.

Age-Friendly NYC began their efforts by soliciting direct feedback from older New York City residents through a series of town halls that were conducted in seven different languages and drew approximately 1,500 older adults and their caregivers.[76] In response to the findings of the assessments, in 2009, the City announced 59 initiatives across 13 city agencies to improve the quality of life for older adults. The city also appointed a Commission for an Age-Friendly NYC to engage private organizations in becoming more inclusive. Some of the results of the initiatives included: making streets safe for older adults to cross, installing more than 1,500 new benches throughout the city, using school buses to drive older people to supermarkets, installing safe, accessible bus stop shelters, and improving access to recreational and cultural activities.[77]

> Age-Friendly NYC has a preventive approach at its core. If we create the right conditions, we can keep people independent and avoid or delay frailty.

The Aging Economy

In her interview, Lindsay Goldman noted that business owners and policy makers must recognize that older adults are a large voting and consumer population. Supporting older individuals and creating inclusive cities and businesses is in the best interests of everyone. From the vantage point of fiscal prudence, keeping people engaged and active slows the trajectory of illness and disability, which reduces the need for city services and social insurance programs.

Multi-sectoral Partnerships

The Age-Friendly NYC Commission members, appointed by the Mayor, represent sectors, including architecture, libraries, technology, urban planning, education, local businesses, and resilience. The Commission also includes the presidents of all five boroughs, the speaker of the City Council, select Council members, and the commissioner of the Department of Aging. Through this multidisciplinary public and private partnership, the Commission works to influence planning, policy, and future initiatives. The Commission also develops toolkits in different languages that contain industry-specific age-friendly recommendations.[78]

An example of one of the public-private partnerships that Lindsay described was a partnership with the Design for Aging Committee[79] of the American Institute of Architects' New York Chapter.[80] Age-Friendly NYC and the Department for the Aging worked with the Design for Aging Committee to produce an aging-in-place guide to educate building owners about low and no-cost improvements to keep older residents healthy and safe and reduce falls risk. Lindsay expressed the need for the overarching concept of "age in everything" because health systems, city designs, and policies that are good for older community members are good for everyone.

Another program that builds age-inclusive communities designed by stakeholders to support social inclusion, purposeful living, and intergenerational connections is Ibasho.

Our focus should be on what we can design to create opportunities for older adults to make a purposeful contribution to the world in the meaningful relationships with people of all ages. (Emi Kiyota)

EMI KIYOTA, M.ARCH, PHD
IBASHO

Emi Kiyota is an environmental gerontologist and the founder and president of Ibasho.[81] She recently completed a Loeb Fellowship at Harvard University and will be participating in an Atlantic fellowship at the Global Brain Health Institute in the University of California San Francisco where she will be studying dementia-inclusive city planning.

Elder Resilience

Ibasho is a Japanese term meaning, "whereabouts" but implying "a place where you feel at home being yourself." Ibasho is built on the belief that elders are a resource, not a burden. The Ibasho cafés serve as a source of connection and support for those most marginalized and each café functions as an evacuation center. Emi stressed that disasters impact older and disabled adults disproportionately.[82,83,84,85] The first Ibasho café was built in 2013 as a form of resilience support in Ofunato, Japan, after the Great East Japan earthquake and tsunami that displaced 65,000 people. The next Ibasho café was built in Barangay Bagong Buhay, Ormoc City, Province of Leyte, Philippines in 2014 after Typhoon Yolanda. The Ibasho community members in Japan funded part of the project and visited the community to offer assistance and guidance. Emi mentioned that the café is changing the local perception of aging by being instrumental in the community recovery. The most recent Ibasho café was built in Kathmandu, Nepal, after the 7.8 magnitude earthquake of 2015 that affected more than 8,000 people.

The café building serves as a tool to develop community capacity and give older residents the opportunity to learn and work together to solve the problem of social isolation.

Bottom-Up Design and Operation

The cafés are designed, built, and operated by the community members of all ages. Emi refers to this as a bottom-up approach that honors the wisdom of all of the community members. The cafés are culturally relevant self-sustaining community hubs that are made possible by coalitions of local community members of all ages, technical experts, government entities, and not-for-profit organizations.

Ibasho Garden in the Philippines

> Making lasting friendships in older age is not common
> and it is profoundly important.

Ibasho community members participate in programs together and are connected by a shared purpose. People of all levels of physical and cognitive abilities are encouraged to spend as much time in the cafés and participate in any community activates that they chose. The activities of each café are individual to their location and the community interest. Some projects include gardening and selling produce, running a noodle house, operating a tea house, growing flowers, selling crafts made by café members, and housing an internet café. Emi expressed the idea that making good friends in older age is not as easy as when we are young. She has witnessed many older adults working together and becoming good friends as a result. Some continue to visit friends after one has moved into a nursing home. They also look out for each other; if one member does not visit the café as usual, their friend will check on them.

Ibasho Café, Japan, Five-Year Anniversary Celebration

Children are good for older people because older people are filled with the spirit of generativity.

Intergenerational Connections

Ibasho café members organize many programs that involve children. In some programs, the older residents act as grandparents and impart love and wisdom. Occasionally, the younger community members participate in the program design. In Nepal, the youth decided to teach the older residents how to read and write. This underlines the importance of involvement of all ages and the understanding that everyone can purposefully contribute to the community.

Our goal is not to only create the building. Our goal is to change social perceptions about aging and the role of elders. We use the building as a tool to develop community capacity because older people have to learn to work together as a group to solve the problem of social isolation.

Ibasho Nepal Vision Workshop

In June 2018, in collaboration with the World Bank and the Asian Development Bank, members of Ibasho Nepal, Japan, and the Philippines met in Ormoc, Philippines, for a peer-to-peer program to exchange learning and determine the provision of inputs. The participants also collaborated to document strategies and best practice. They also shared with technical experts and development partners emerging lessons from the implementation of Ibasho activities and research findings from the three countries. The symposium presented opportunities for elders to build cross-cultural support networks. It also provided the space and incentive for technical experts to reimagine the role of elders when designing physical and social infrastructures.

Emi Kiyota opening the 2018 Peer-to-Peer Exchange Program

Some of the most memorable quotes from the peer-to-peer exchange meeting include:

- "The beauty of Ibasho is that disaster brought us together and unleashed our potential to build the community that we have become." (Ibasho Nepal)

- "It was difficult to rise up and recover our life again. We lost properties, friends, family members. Ibasho played a huge part in helping them stand again and live a normal life." (Ibasho Japan)

- "We have to continue and move forward. We are grateful for Emi Kiyota and Ibasho for helping us not be left behind by transforming us to become productive members of the society. Respect towards the elders, especially from the younger generations in The Philippines, is fading. Because of Ibasho projects like recycling of plastics, we are proof that elders are also useful members of the society."

Ibasho members from Nepal, Japan, and the Philippines Sharing their skills and knowledge

Emi hopes to broaden the idea of Ibasho cafés to Ibasho villages, where community members use existing community resources to create community hubs throughout the village. Examples Emi gave include building an internet café in an existing senior residence, making private libraries available to all, and using existing buildings to house community activities.

An Ibasho Phillippines member talking about her experience of developing the Ibasho Philippines. The Ibasho Philippines Elders composed the quote printed on her blouse.

Timebanking

Another example of using existing community resources to promote social inclusion is timebanking.[86] Edgar Cahn founded the concept of timebanking in 1980 as a response to governmental policy that lessened support for social programs.[87] He is the author of two books on timebanking: *Time Dollars: The New Currency that Enables Americans to Turn Their Hidden Resource-Time-Into Personal Security & Community Renewal* and *No More Throw-Away People*. Timebanks are an organized method for individuals to donate their time by exchanging skills or teaching to a community member and receive skills or teaching from the same or another community member in return.[88] Timebanks are based on the theory of Co-Production[89] where the person receiving will also be contributing, which creates equality among community members.

linkAges timebank cuts across social categories, including income status, education, and ethnicity. Loneliness affects every demographic and social strata. (Dr. Paul Tang)

PAUL TANG
LINKAGES[90]

At the time of his interview, Dr. Paul Tang was the Director of the David Druker Center for Health Systems Innovation. Today he is the Vice President and Chief Health Transformation Officer at IBM Watson Health.

The David Druker Center for Health Systems Innovation designs and implements programs to support community health and well-being that are based on the Center's core beliefs that:

- Health is more than health care;
- Each community member has the ability to contribute to the health of other community members;
- It is imperative that health systems collaborate with communities to meet the individual needs of their patients.[91]

One of the programs of the David Druker Center for Health Systems Innovation is the linkAges timebank network that facilitates purposeful intergenerational connections and valuable social support systems within existing communities. The name linkAges stands for linking across the ages.

We are enhancing the resilience of families and communities by increasing a sense of well-being and happiness in the community.

A multidisciplinary team of physicians, clinicians, an ethnographer, and administrators designed the linkAges timebank model. The ethnographer conducted a series of interviews with older adults to learn what prevented them from living life as fully as they wished. The two main barriers the interviews revealed were isolation and loneliness. One interviewee said, "As you age, your world dies before you do." That information was the inspiration for the linkAges timebanks.

The world goes around because people can and do share with other people who have needs or would like to enrich their lives by learning something new.

Lifelong Learning

Paul Tang mentioned that members in the linkAges communities exchange tasks such as organizational and housekeeping projects, skills sharing, and transportation. Most trades, however, are those for enrichment by learning a new skill or hobby such as technology or photography.

Technology instruction at linkAges timebank exchange

We are seeing the very cross-generational exchange and
learning that you would like to see in a cultured society.
We are rebuilding community.

Intergenerational Connections

The linkAges timebanks are comprised of all generations with one third
over age 65, one third between 50 and 64, and one third younger than
50. Most of the exchanges for members over 50 occur with a younger
community member.

Social services create a natural form of prevention.

Upstream Health Prevention and Resilience

Paul mentioned that the healthcare costs in the US are high, while the quality outcomes rank last among developed nations. He believes that America can learn from other countries that invest in social services to prevent illness. The American system could be referred to as sick care as opposed to health care because the system is far more heavily based in treating illness and injury after it has occurred rather than preventing both. He asserts that health care influences only 10 percent of total health outcomes.[92]

Can we increase the percentage of those living healthy independent lives by one percent?

Because of the high cost of the "super utilizer" patients who are responsible for most of the healthcare spending in America, many insurers and providers are dedicated to building systems that serve this cohort better and at a lower cost.[93] Paul noted that 5 percent of the population is responsible for 50 percent of the health care spend. Paul's unique perspective is focused further upstream on the 95 percent of the population, with an eye toward prevention. The David Druker Center for Health Systems Innovation has the goal of increasing the 95 percent to 96 and preventing 1 percent of the population from entering the "super utilizer" cohort. They believe that loneliness prevention and productive engagement in communities across the country has the potential to move that needle one tick. With a population of more than 326 million, the value could be significant.

Providers should be compensated for improving the
health status of the community they serve.

Paul believes that, due to the political nature surrounding social services in America, the private sector and healthcare providers bear the responsibility of community-based social service delivery. linkAges timebanks have the potential to be a benefit to any health system seeking to take on that mission. Today the linkAges timebanks are operational in the San Francisco Bay and Santa Cruz areas of Northern California. The Center plans to expand linkAges into Sacramento, California, next. The timebanks are open to individuals, organizations, and health systems.

The innovations for social inclusion for people of all ages and abilities in this chapter are a guiding light for how we must envision older adults in our community in the world—as assets of strength, insight, and purpose. We hope this chapter leaves the reader with a broader vision of health and well-being and the drive to advocate for social inclusion for people of all ages and abilities.

The full interviews referenced in this chapter can be found at this link: www. accessh.org/agingwell.

11

Eight Lessons for Social Inclusion and High-Quality Sustainable Elder Care

The inspiration for this book is derived from our commitment to the belief that sharing best practice is an essential tool to guide societies and health systems to make the adaptations needed to support the growing aging population. The case studies and interviews portray initiatives, programs, and health system innovations that can contribute to making the adaptations successful and greatly contribute to the well-being of older adults.

One of the greatest stories of the 20th century was that we doubled the life expectancy of adults. Now we need to make sure we have all the supports in place to assure not just a long life but a high quality of that long life.[1] (Terry Fulmer, president of the John A. Hartford Foundation)

Many of the best practices that we describe were fueled by or made possible by value-based reimbursement policy. Value includes lower costs, better health outcomes, including patient satisfaction, more access to care, and improved patient well-being. In the preceding chapters, we have seen reoccurring themes that are integral to many of the programs and initiatives that we documented.

Here we distill our findings into eight lessons for delivery of high-quality sustainable elder care and support and creating communities of social inclusion.

Lesson One: The Availability of Affordable Long-Term Care Insurance Is Essential to Improve Access to Care for Older Adults

Sadly, many people in the United States cannot afford health care. Older people are especially vulnerable because they use the health system the most and often cannot afford the co-payments. Additionally, Medicare does not cover dental or vision care, which leads to other health complications and impediments to well-being. The long-term care insurance industry was faced with sustainability challenges early on but has recovered in recent years, leaving higher premiums that are unaffordable by most. This is problematic because most people will need long-term care in their lifetime. The costs of such care can leave family members and the surviving spouse in poverty.

Lesson Two: Person-Centered Care Is a Vital Component of High-Quality Care and for Older Adults

Long-term care providers are committing to person-centered care by embracing a more horizontal culture of teamwork steeped in the respect for the dignity of older adults. Culture change is necessary but difficult.

The board, the management, and all of the staff must embrace it or it will not be sustainable. On first glance, one would think that person-centered policies require more staff and result in higher costs, but our research has shown the opposite.

We found examples of excellence in long-term care at St. John's and Beatitudes Campus with care partners who work as a team and do not rotate. Allen Power brought the person-centered care concept to dementia with the belief that those with dementia should not be seg-regated. He also asserts that person-centered approaches can often be used instead of antipsychotic medications. The Eden Alternative phi-losophy that is based in the well-being and dignity of older adults is the basis for culture change and organizational transformation that leads to person-centered policies and practices in institutional and home care.

Lesson Three: Palliative Care and Social Support in the Home Is Essential to High-Quality Elder Care

The trend toward delivering health care and social supports in the home and community is growing. Most people 65 and older are living with chronic illnesses, making primary and palliative care one in the same for that population. Home-based primary and palliative care can offer a better option to the expensive cycle of emergency department (ED) visits, hospitalizations, and skilled nursing stays that are dangerous and stressful to older adults. Additionally, insurers and providers are increasingly understanding the importance of involving the patient and the family in the care plan. Health delivery systems are reorganizing and insurers are reshaping reimbursement policy to honor the late life wishes of patients.

The Independence at Home demonstration project of Northwell Health, led by Dr. Kristofer Smith, is a glowing example of how to deliver home-based primary care to the most frail older adults that greatly improves their quality of life, honors their late life care plan, and substantially lowers the cost of care. We hope that the demon-stration project will influence the Centers for Medicare and Medicaid to reimburse for Independence at Home programs and make them available to many.

Under the direction of Dr. Diane E. Meier, the Center to Advance Palliative Care has increased awareness of the large care gap that palliative care can fill—especially when delivered in all settings. The Center to Advance Palliative is also committed to encouraging all clinicians to receive geriatric care training.

Some providers, such as Dr. Allan Teel, who are enabling their patients to age in place, connect those patients to the existing services and social supports that are available in their community. Involving the community in the daily life of older individuals makes sense. It divides the "care" burden while enabling the individual to maintain meaning-ful connections socially and to receive other supportive services such as meals, assistance with activities of daily living, and transportation.

Lesson Four: Coordinated Primary Health Care Is Essential to High-Quality Elder Care

Coordinated, accessible primary care can yield better health outcomes and reduce redundant and unnecessary care. Coordinated primary care is especially effective for older individuals living with comorbidities who are receiving care in many settings and by multiple clinicians.

Dr. Erik Langhoff of the James J. Peters Veterans Health Admin-istration demonstrated that coordinated primary care is most effective with the use of technology in care coordination across multiple spe-cialties, electronic health record maintenance, diagnostics, telemedicine, and outcome measurement.

The patient-centered medical home model is an example of accessible and coordinated primary care that, according to Drs. Erin Giovannetti and Michael Barr with the National Committee for Quality Assurance

(NCQA), can produce better health outcomes, improved patient satisfaction, and reduced care costs. NCQA is recognizing an ever-increasing number of patient-centered medical homes as providers and insurers understand the benefits.

Lesson Five: Delivery of Acute and Hospital-Level Care in the Home and Community Can Lower Healthcare Costs and Improve Access and Well-Being for Older Adults

Emergency department and hospital care is the most expensive care. Older adults use the ED and are hospitalized more than any other cohort. They are also more likely to experience adverse health events, misdiagnosis, functional and cognitive decline, and medical error in both settings. One way to address this issue and significantly lower the cost of care is to provide hospital-level and emergency care at home and in the community.

ACUTE CARE

Older adults prefer to receive acute care in their homes and avoid the emotional stress of riding in an ambulance to the ED and potential subsequent hospital admission. DispatchHealth is proof that it is possible to treat acute health episodes in the home. The model, detailed by Kevin Riddleberger and Dr. Mark Prather, uses sophisticated portable diagnostic equipment and employs clinicians who are more highly trained than emergency medical technicians. DispatchHealth providers have access to the patient electronic health record system and update them in real time. The DispatchHealth team is meeting the need for acute care in senior residence communities with all levels of care. Insurers have begun to reimburse acute care in the home and community because it has shown to produce impressive cost savings, better health outcomes, greatly improved access to care, and much higher rates of patient satisfaction. DispatchHealth estimates that they have generated more than US$25 million in cost savings since the inception of the company.

ACUTE AND PALLIATIVE CARE

Call9 is filling the acute and palliative care gap for older adults living in skilled nursing homes by providing around-the-clock technology-enabled specialized and personalized care in nursing homes. They are also enabling their patients to die with dignity in the location of their choice and with care that is aligned with the priorities of the patient and the family. Their model drastically cuts healthcare costs for their patients and improves access and patient satisfaction.

HOSPITAL CARE

Hospital-level care in the home, such as the Hospital at Home program led by Dr. Bruce Leff, produces higher levels of patient satisfaction and the same or better health outcomes at one third of the cost. Patients in the emergency department who meet certain criteria are transported back to their home and given care there. It is likely that the demonstration projects of this model will compel the Centers for Medicare and Medicaid Services and other insurers to make hospital care at home available through bundled payment reimbursements, enabling a larger-scale adoption in the United States.

Lesson Six: Dementia Presents Challenges and Opportunities for High-Quality Care and Caregiver Support

CAREGIVING

The burden of caregiving for those living with dementia is often borne by the informal caregiver. As shown by Dr. Mary Mittelman of the NYU Caregiver Intervention, the value of supporting the caregiver cannot be underestimated in regard to both cost of care and well-being. Jed Levine described the commitment of CaringKind to ensuring that all individuals who are caring for people with dementia receive specific training and education because the disease presents unique challenges. Those with dementia often wish to walk around outside. As described by Elizabeth Santiago, when they become lost, there are low-tech programs to find them that can be easily and inexpensively implemented by institutions anywhere. The Wanderer's Safety Program is one such program.

INSTITUTIONAL SETTINGS

Those living with dementia respond to the built environment differently. Dr. Davina Porock led efforts by institutions to use colors and visual cues that make the environments safer and more accessible. Davina described that emergency departments, hospitals, and long-term care providers are also learning that moving people with dementia from location to location can cause further disorientation and discomfort.

Tena Alonzo and Karen Mitchell of Beatitudes Campus and Rebecca Priest with St. John's Home are creating home-like environments without the use of overhead announcement systems, alarms, and chemical or physical restraints. The environments often include animals, gardens, large common areas, and furniture (including beds) that are the same furniture one would find in non-institutional homes. To reduce clinical environmental cues further and to empower long-term care residents, most of the staff of St. John's does not wear uniforms.

In both long-term care residences, the staff is also encouraged to build meaningful relationships with the residents and their families. These relationships support the dignity of risk decisions such as whether to continue with medications that have unpleasant side effects or whether to allow a family member to walk around outside.

BEHAVIORS

It would benefit caregivers and clinicians to understand that, because those living with dementia cannot communicate with words, they communicate with their actions. Dr. Allen Power, Tena Alonzo, Karen Mitchell, and Rebecca Priest support the fact that behaviors that convey unhappiness and aggravation express an unmet need. Those actions are far too often treated with antipsychotic medications and labeled as "resisting care."

Rebecca Priest and her team employ person-centered methods to identify the individual needs being expressed by their residents and design novel approaches to meet those needs. They also educate the staff and residents about the life and interests of their residents who are living with dementia. This enables everyone to see the person before his or her memory challenge. The methods of St. John's have been so successful that those who are living with dementia are able to live in community rather than in segregated areas.

Like everyone else, people with dementia have individual rhythms and habits. They do not like to live on someone else's schedule. They are not happy when they are woken up earlier than they wish, are served food when they are not hungry that they do not like, and are forced to participate in activities that they do not find enjoyable. They also do not want to be locked inside day and night. This displeasure can lead to aggressive or unpleasant behavior and, when expressed in the late afternoon, is labeled as sundowning. Under the guidance of Tena Alonzo and Karen Mitchell, the team of Beatitudes Campus has become so adept at understanding the individual needs, preferences, and rhythms of residents with dementia that they have ended all cases of sundowning in their memory care residences. They embrace liberalized diets and are so organizationally adaptive that they are able to allow residents to live on their own schedules.

PALLIATIVE CARE

Person-centered palliative care for those living with dementia that is focused on the comfort of the patient is slowly being embraced throughout America. The model has shown to be beneficial on an institutional and organizational level while supporting the well-being of the person living with dementia. We hope that Comfort Matters™ will eventually spread to countries outside of the United States and become the standard level of dementia care we come to expect.

STIGMA

We applaud the efforts of organizations such as the Dementia Action Alliance and people like Jackie and Lon Pinkowitz and Karen Love who are dedicated to confronting the stigma of those living with dementia. Caring Conversations is a simple and impactful method of convening individuals from all walks of life and in multiple professions with those living with dementia in their community. These conversations can help people see the person before his or her cognitive challenge. Rather than the deficit-based view, the whole person vision of someone who is living with dementia can have profound and lasting change on how we move forward as a society to support and embrace those with the disease.

Brian LeBlanc is living proof that people living with dementia are powerful advocates and experts. He, Lindsay Goldman of Age-Friendly

NYC, and Mia Oberlink of the AdvantAge Initiative understand that those living with dementia must be involved in all levels of policy making that deal with dementia. Doing otherwise only furthers the stigma.

Lesson Seven: It Is Imperative for Health Systems to Provide Both Social and Medical Supports with Preventative Interventions That Address the Social Determinants of Health

Healthcare systems around the world, and most definitely the United States, need to make efforts further upstream with robust health prevention as social support measures that address the social determinants of health and treat the whole person, including biopsychosocial needs. This population health concept has the potential to reduce health system costs and contribute to the well-being of all people. It is the only way forward to care for the aging population effectively and sustainably.

PREVENTION AND CARE TRANSITIONS

Evidence-based chronic disease self-management and health prevention programs, such as those described by the Partners in Care Foundation founder June Simmons, have proven to be impactful on health outcomes and healthcare costs. Additionally, employing varying levels of clinical care and social supports can enable a safe transition from the hospital directly to the home that greatly improves patient well-being and lowers healthcare costs.

FUNCTION

Under the leadership of Sarah Szanton, the CAPABLE program is proof positive that it is possible to combine social and medical supports to improve the functional capacities of the most frail, community-dwelling older adults. Sarah taught us that goal-oriented, restorative care is most effective when the goals of the program participant are honored as the top priority because people are more willing to challenge themselves to meet a goal that is meaningful to them.

Lesson Eight: Social Inclusion and the Opportunity to Live a Purposeful Life Are Essential to the Happiness and Well-Being of Older Adults

Social inclusion represents upstream physical and mental health prevention. Inclusion can delay frailty and mitigate loneliness, isolation, and depression. Social inclusion also helps dispel the stigma of aging. Public and private organizations and communities are building inclusive and accessible environments for older people. Some community members have joined together to build socially connected hubs where people of all ages can remain engaged and supported.

Dr. Paul Tang and his team at linkAges created one such hub in the model of a timebank where community members help each other out on a trade basis. Physicians in the Sutter Health practice can write a prescription for timebanking when they see the need for social inclusion. This is a fine example of providing both health and social support under the same roof.

Emi Kiyota leads Ibasho as they support the development of community-led social hubs called cafés. The three cafés around the world serve as a form of community resilience after natural disasters. They are community-run, self-sustaining meeting places for people of all ages and abilities.

HOUSING

Housing can enrich the lives of older adults through multigenerational connections, inclusive built environments, and lifelong learning. Communities such as St. John's and Beatitudes Campus that provide space and support for older adults to create their own clubs and civic activities built on their life experience and passions send a strong message that older individuals still have much to give and can have lasting impact on the younger generation, their community, and all levels of policy.

As shown by the naturally occurring retirement communities and the Village to Village movement, there are many successful examples of neighborhoods whose members joined together to receive social supports and services and health care collectively in the community. These communities will likely continue to grow with the aging population.

Joani Blank was an older person who embraced community living in the form of cohousing. Cohousing structures are designed to enhance community inclusion and productive cooperation with shared spaces and shared meals and projects. The multigenerational nature of cohousing enables fellow residents to form meaningful relationships with their neighbors of all ages.

Led by Anne Doyle, Lasell Village was designed with the dedication to lifelong learning and intergenerational connections. The retirement community is on the campus of Lasell College and supports continual opportunities for lifelong learning at the college and in the community. Lasell Village is also home to a nursery school. Some residents volunteer at the school, and others enjoy the children involved in their daily activities throughout Village.

AGE-INCLUSIVE CITIES

Led by Lindsay Goldman, Age-Friendly NYC is proof that environments that are accessible to people of all ages and abilities are stronger, more resilient, and more economically secure. Older community members must be involved in all stages of planning and implementing age-inclusive initiatives. This was especially impactful with the early efforts of Age-Friendly NYC when they conducted town halls around the city to learn directly from older individuals what was needed to make the city accessible and to enable them to live engaged productive lives. Lindsay Goldman asserts that, to have the greatest impact and remain sustainable, age-inclusive planning should also include public and private entities from a variety of sectors while remaining true to the mantra of "Age in Everything."

An important aspect of inclusive cities is the availability for older people to remain active in the workforce in whatever capacity they desire or need. Employment keeps people engaged as productive members of society. It also keeps them socially and physically active. In many cases employment enables older adults to earn much needed income. Older adults also help fill the growing workforce shortage. Under the leadership of Ruth Finkelstein, the Age Smart Employer initiative seeks to honor employers who are able to attract and retain older employees through training, job modification, creating mentor-type relationships, and offering part-time employment and step-down retirement options.

Including individuals of all ages in civic and community life helps to dispel the harmful stigma of aging. Through the program, Exceeding Expectations, Ruth Finkelstein and journalist Dorian Block use storytelling to dispel the aging stigma. They profile a cross section of adults in New York City who have lived longer than the life expectancy of the city and are living vibrant active lives.

Looking Forward

The US might not be the first country one would expect to find exceptional care and support for older adults. We were pleasantly surprised to find such examples ourselves. The only way around the existing, inefficient, and expensive health system is with an innovative pioneering spirit that many Americans still hold dear. It is with disappointment that we must acknowledge that the models of excellence are the exception and not the rule. We are encouraged by our research that this is changing, albeit slowly.

We hope that this book serves as inspiration and incentive to health providers and those dedicated to optimal aging and well-being of older adults around the world. We believe, however, that the strongest and most lasting transformations will be driven by the stakeholders—the older adults who, as baby boomers, changed almost every system they touched from their active civic engagement to their demand for convenience and person-centered service. We have seen that excellence is possible and must all unite to make it standard practice.

Additional Reading

We would like to mention that our office in Sweden conducted a series of interviews with similar focus areas, including long-term care, care coordination, mobile health, home health, person-centered care, caregiver support, technology, dementia care, and housing models for those living with dementia. The interviews have been distilled into takeaways and analyses that are available in a new book entitled *Aging with Dignity*. The book will be available on Amazon soon. More information on *Aging with Dignity* can be found at this link: http://accessh.org/agingwithdignity/

Appendix—Indicators List: Essential Elements of an Elder Friendly Community

Percentage of People Age 65+ Who Report Their Community Is a Good Place to Live

ADDRESSES BASIC NEEDS

- Affordable housing is available to community residents

    1. Percentage of people age 65+ who spend >30%/≤30% of their income on housing

    2. Percentage of people age 65+ who want to remain in their current residence and are confident they will be able to afford to do so

- Housing is modified to accommodate mobility and safety

    1. Percentage of householders age 65+ in housing units with home modification needs

- The neighborhood is livable and safe

    1. Percentage of people age 65+ who feel safe/unsafe in their neighborhood

    2. Percentage of people age 65+ who report few/multiple problems in the neighborhood

    3. Percentage of people age 65+ who are satisfied with the neighborhood as a place to live

- People have enough to eat

    1. Percentage of people age 65+ who report cutting the size of or skipping meals due to lack of money

- Assistance services are available and residents know how to access them

    1. Percentage of people age 65+ who do not know whom to call if they need information about services in their community

    2. Percentage of people age 65+ who are aware/unaware of selected services in their community

    3. Percentage of people age 65+ with adequate assistance in ADL and/or IADL activities

OPTIMIZES PHYSICAL AND MENTAL HEALTH AND WELL-BEING

- Community promotes and provides access to necessary and preventive health services

    1. Rates of screening and vaccination for various conditions among people 65+

2. Percentage of people age 65+ who thought they needed the help of a healthcare professional because they felt depressed or anxious and have not seen one (for those symptoms)

3. Percentage of people age 65+ whose physical or mental health interfered with their activities in the past month

4. Percentage of people age 65+ who report being in good to excellent health

- Opportunities for physical activity are available and used

    1. Percentage of people age 65+ who participate in regular physical exercise

- Obstacles to use of necessary medical care are minimized

    1. Percentage of people age 65+ with a usual source of care

    2. Percentage of people age 65+ who failed to obtain needed medical care

    3. Percentage of people age 65+ who had problems paying for medical care

    4. Percentage of people age 65+ who had problems paying for prescription drugs

    5. Percentage of people age 65+ who had problems paying for dental care or eyeglasses

- Palliative care services are available and advertised

    1. Percentage of people age 65+ who know whether palliative care services are available

MAXIMIZES INDEPENDENCE FOR THE FRAIL AND DISABLED

- Transportation is accessible and affordable

    1. Percentage of people age 65+ who have access to public transportation

- The community service system enables people to live comfortably and safely at home

    1. Percentage of people age 65+ with adequate assistance in activities of daily living (ADL)

    2. Percentage of people age 65+ with adequate assistance in instrumental activities of daily living (IADL)

- Caregivers are mobilized to complement the formal service system

    1. Percentage of people age 65+ who provide help to the frail or disabled

    2. Percentage of people age 65+ who get respite/relief from their caregiving activity

PROMOTES SOCIAL AND CIVIC ENGAGEMENT

- Residents maintain connections with friends and neighbors

    1. Percentage of people age 65+ who socialized with friends or neighbors in the past week

- Civic, cultural, religious, and recreational activities include older residents

  1. Percentage of people age 65+ who attended church, temple, or other in the past week

  2. Percentage of people age 65+ who attended movies, sports events, clubs, or group events in the past week

  3. Percentage of people age 65+ who engaged in at least one social, religious, or cultural activity in the past week

- Opportunities for volunteer work are readily available

  1. Percentage of people age 65+ who participate in volunteer work

- Community residents help and trust each other

  1. Percentage of people age 65+ who live in "helping communities"

- Appropriate work is available to those who want it

  1. Percentage of people age 65+ who would like to be working for pay

Indicators List: Essential Elements of an Elder Friendly Community

Percentage of people age 65+ who report their community is a good place to live

ADDRESSES BASIC NEEDS
- **Affordable housing is available to community residents**
  1. Percentage of people age 65+ who spend >30%/≤30% of their income on housing
  2. Percentage of people age 65+ who want to remain in their current residence and are confident they will be able to afford to do so
- **Housing is modified to accommodate mobility and safety**
  3. Percentage of householders age 65+ in housing units with home modification needs
- **The neighborhood is livable and safe**
  4. Percentage of people age 65+ who feel safe/unsafe in their neighborhood
  5. Percentage of people age 65+ who report few/multiple problems in the neighborhood
  6. Percentage of people age 65+ who are satisfied with the neighborhood as a place to live
- **People have enough to eat**
  7. Percentage of people age 65+ who report cutting the size of or skipping meals due to lack of money
- **Assistance services are available and residents know how to access them**
  8. Percentage of people age 65+ who do not know whom to call if they need information about services in their community
  9. Percentage of people age 65+ who are aware/unaware of selected services in their community
  10. Percentage of people age 65+ with adequate assistance in ADL and/or IADL activities

OPTIMIZES PHYSICAL AND MENTAL HEALTH AND WELL-BEING
- **Community promotes and provides access to necessary and preventive health services**
  11. Rates of screening and vaccination for various conditions among people 65+
  12. Percentage of people age 65+ who thought they needed the help of a healthcare professional because they felt depressed or anxious and have not seen one (for those symptoms)
  13. Percentage of people age 65+ whose physical or mental health interfered with their activities in the past month
  14. Percentage of people age 65+ who report being in good to excellent health
- **Opportunities for physical activity are available and used**
  15. Percentage of people age 65+ who participate in regular physical exercise
- **Obstacles to use of necessary medical care are minimized**
  16. Percentage of people age 65+ with a usual source of care
  17. Percentage of people age 65+ who failed to obtain needed medical care
  18. Percentage of people age 65+ who had problems paying for medical care
  19. Percentage of people age 65+ who had problems paying for prescription drugs
  20. Percentage of people age 65+ who had problems paying for dental care or eyeglasses
- **Palliative care services are available and advertised**
  21. Percentage of people age 65+ who know whether palliative care services are available

MAXIMIZES INDEPENDENCE FOR THE FRAIL AND DISABLED
- **Transportation is accessible and affordable**
  22. Percentage of people age 65+ who have access to public transportation
- **The community service system enables people to live comfortably and safely at home**
  23. Percentage of people age 65+ with adequate assistance in activities of daily living (ADL)
  24. Percentage of people age 65+ with adequate assistance in instrumental activities of daily living (IADL)
- **Caregivers are mobilized to complement the formal service system**
  25. Percentage of people age 65+ who provide help to the frail or disabled
  26. Percentage of people age 65+ who get respite/relief from their caregiving activity

PROMOTES SOCIAL AND CIVIC ENGAGEMENT
- **Residents maintain connections with friends and neighbors**
  27. Percentage of people age 65+ who socialized with friends or neighbors in the past week
- **Civic, cultural, religious, and recreational activities include older residents**
  28. Percentage of people age 65+ who attended church, temple, or other in the past week
  29. Percentage of people age 65+ who attended movies, sports events, clubs, or group events in the past week
  30. Percentage of people age 65+ who engaged in at least one social, religious, or cultural activity in the past week
- **Opportunities for volunteer work are readily available**
  31. Percentage of people age 65+ who participate in volunteer work
- **Community residents help and trust each other**
  32. Percentage of people age 65+ who live in "helping communities"
- **Appropriate work is available to those who want it**
  33. Percentage of people age 65+ who would like to be working for pay

Center for Home Care Policy and Research
Visiting Nurse Service of New York

ADVANTAGE The
Initiative

End Notes

Chapter 1

1. World Health Organization (2015). Global strategy and action plan.
2. Bongaarts, J. (2009). Human population growth and the demographic transition. *Philosophical transactions of the Royal Society of London,* 364(1532), 2985–2990.
3. (2014). The next America. America's morphing age pyramid. Pew Research Center. http://www.pewresearch.org/next-america/age-pyramid/. Accessed March 2016.
4. National Institute on Aging. Why population aging matters: A global perspective. Trend 3: rising numbers of the oldest old. https://www.nia. nih. gov/publication/why-population-aging-matters-global-perspective/ trend3-rising-numbers-oldest-old. Accessed January 10, 2016.
5. Ibid.
6. United Nations, Department of Economic and Social Affairs, Population Division (2015). World Population Ageing 2015 (ST/ESA/SER.A/390).

Chapter 2

1. OECD. Health at a glance. How does the United States compare? https://www.oecd.org/unitedstates/Health-at-a-Glance-2015-Key-Findings-UNITED-STATES.pdf. Accessed April 2017.

2.   Ibid.
3.   Institute for Healthcare Improvement. IHI Triple Aim Initiative. Better care for individuals. Better health for populations, and lower per capita costs. http://www.ihi.org/Engage/Initiatives/TripleAim/Pages/default. aspx. Accessed April 2017.
4.   Aldridge, M.D. & Kelley, A.S. (2015). The myth regarding the high cost of end-of-life care. *American Journal of Public Health*, 105(12), 2411–2415.
5.   Emanuel, E.J. (2012). Where are the health care cost savings. *JAMA*, 307(1), 39–40.
6.   Koller, C.F. & Khullar, D. (2017). Primary care spending rate—A lever for encouraging investment in primary care. *New England Journal of Medicine*, 377(18), 1709–1711.
7.   Squires, D. & Anderson, C. (2015). Issues in international health policy. US healthcare from a global perspective: Spending, use of services, prices, and health in 13 countries. The Commonwealth Fund. http:// www. commonwealthfund.org/~/media/files/publications/issuebrief/2015/ oct/1819_squires_us_hlt_care_global_perspective_oecd_ intl_brief_v3.pdf. Accessed October 2017.
8.   Osborn, R., Squires, D., Doty, M.M., Sarnak, D.O., & Schneider, E.C. (2016). In new survey of eleven countries, US adults still struggle with access to and affordability of healthcare. *Health Affairs*, 35(12), 2327–2336.
9.   Sasson, C., Wiler, J.L., Haukoos, J.S., Sklar, D., Kellermann, A.L., Beck, D., Urbina, C., Heilpern, K., & Magid, D.J. (2012). The changing landscape of America's health care system and the value of emergency medicine. *Academic Emergency Medicine*, 19(10), 1204–1211.
10. OECD. Health at a glance. How does the United States compare? https://www.oecd.org/unitedstates/Health-at-a-Glance-2015-Key-Findings-UNITED-STATES.pdf. Accessed April 2017.
11. Commonwealth Fund (2014). US health system ranks last among eleven countries on measures of access, equity, quality, efficiency, and healthy lives. http://www.commonwealthfund.org/publications/press-releases/2014/jun/us-health-system-ranks-last. Accessed April 2017.

12. Commonwealth Fund (2014). Mirror mirror on the wall, 2014 update: How the US health care system compares internationally. http://www. commonwealthfund.org/publications/fund-reports/2014/jun/mirror-mirror. Accessed May 2017.

13. Institute of Medicine (2008). Retooling for an aging America: building the health care workforce. *National Academies Press*.

14. Olivero, M. (2015). Doctor shortage: Who will take care of the elderly? *US News*. http://health.usnews.com/health-news/patient-advice/ articles/2015/04/21/doctor-shortage-who-will-take-care-of-the-elderly. Accessed April 2017.

15. World Health Organization. Health workforce for ageing populations. http://www.who.int/ageing/publications/health-workforce-ageing-pop-ulations.pdf?ua=1. Accessed April 2017.

16. Sorbero, M.E. (2012). Addressing the geriatrician shortage may help reduce costs without compromising quality. Rand Corporation. http:// www.rand.org/blog/2012/08/addressing-the-geriatrician-shortage-mayhelp-reduce.html. Accessed April 2017.

17. Ibid.

18. US Department of Health and Human Services (2010). Multiple chronic conditions: A strategic framework: Optimum health and quality of life for individuals with multiple chronic conditions. https://www. hhs.gov/ sites/default/files/ash/initiatives/mcc/mcc_framework.pdf. Accessed June 2017.

19. The Lewin Group (2010). Individuals living in the community with chronic conditions and functional limitations: A closer look. Office of the Assistant Secretary for Planning & Evaluation. United States Department of Health and Human Services.

20. US Department of Health and Human Services. About the multiple chronic conditions initiative. https://www.hhs.gov/ash/about-ash/ multiple-chronic-conditions/about-mcc/. Accessed January 2017.

21. Ibid.

22. Chen, C.Y., Thorsteinsdottir, B., Cha, S.S., Hanson, G.J., Peterson, S.M., Rahman, P.A., Naessens, J.M., & Takahashi, P.Y. (2015). Health care outcomes and advance care planning in older adults who receive

home-based palliative care: A pilot cohort study. *Journal of Palliative Medicine*, 18(1), 38–44.

23. UN.org. World Population Aging 1950–2050. Chapter IV. https://unesdoc.org/ark:/48223/pf0000125754. Accessed June 2017.

24. National Institute on Aging. Why population aging matters: A global prospective. Trend 3: Rising numbers of the oldest old. https://www.nia.nih.gov/publication/why-population-aging-matters-global-perspective/trend-3-rising-numbers-oldest-old. Accessed June 2017.

25. World Health Organization (2014). "Ageing well" must be a global priority. http://www.who.int/mediacentre/news/releases/2014/lancet-ageingseries/en/. Accessed February 2017.

26. Chan, A. (2011). 75% of people with dementia may be undiagnosed: Report. *Huffington Post*. http://www.huffingtonpost.com/2011/09/14/dementia-undiagnosed-world_n_960210.html. Accessed April 2017.

27. Dementia statistics. Numbers of people with dementia. Alzheimer's Disease International. https://www.alz.co.uk/research/statistics. Accessed April 2017.

28. Ibid.

29. Ibid.

30. Alzheimer's Association, (2016). 2016 Alzheimer's disease facts and figures. Pg. 17.

31. Ibid.

32. Benjamin, R.M. (2010). Multiple chronic conditions: A public health challenge. *Public Health Reports*, 125(5), 626–627.

33. Centers for Medicare and Medicaid Services (2016). CMS quality strategy 2016. https://www.cms.gov/medicare/quality-initiatives-patient-assessment-instruments/qualityinitiativesgeninfo/downloads/cms-quality-strategy.pdf. Accessed March 2017.

34. Benjamin, R.M. (2010). Multiple chronic conditions: A public health challenge. *Public Health Reports*, 125(5), 626–627.

35. Gerteis, J., Izrael, D., Deitz, D., LeRoy, L., Ricciardi, R., Miller, T. & Basu, J. (2014). Multiple chronic conditions chartbook. Agency for Healthcare Research and Quality, Publications No, Q14-0038. https:// www.ahrq.gov/sites/default/files/wysiwyg/professionals/

preventionchronic-care/decision/mcc/mccchartbook.pdf. Accessed
March 2017.

36. Centers for Medicare & Medicaid Services (2012). Chronic conditions
among Medicare beneficiaries, chartbook 2012. https://www.cms.gov/
Research-Statistics-Data-and-Systems/Statistics-Trends-and-Reports/
Chronic-Conditions/2012ChartBook.html. Accessed March 2017.

37. The American Geriatrics Society Expert Panel on Person-Centered
Care (2015). Person-centered care: A definition and Essential Elements.
Journal of the American Geriatrics Society. https://doi.org/10.1111/
jgs.13866. Accessed November 2016.

38. Institute of Medicine (2001). Crossing the quality chasm: A new
health system for the 21st century. http://nationalacademies.org/
hmd/~/media/ Files/Reportpercent20Files/2001/Crossing-the-
Quality-Chasm/litypercent20Chasmpercent202001percent20percent20
reportpercent20brief.pdf. Accessed December 2016.

39. World Health Organization (2013). Towards people-centered health
systems: An innovative approach for better health outcomes. http://www.
euro.who.int/__data/assets/pdf_file/0006/186756/Towards-peoplecentred-
health-systems-an-innovative-approach-for-better-healthoutcomes.pdf.
Accessed December 2016.

40. Colligan, E.M., Ewald, E., Ruiz, S., Spafford, M., Cross-Barnet, C., &
Parashuram, S. (2017). Innovative oncology care models improve end-
of-life quality, reduce utilization and spending. *Health Affairs*, (36)3,
400–440.

41. Committee on Approaching Death: Addressing Key End of Life Issues;
Institute of Medicine (2015). Dying in America: Improving quality and
honoring individual preferences near the end of life. *National Academies
Press*. Chapter 2.

42. Tabbush, V., Coulourides Kogan, A., Mosqueda, L., & Kominski, G.
(2016). Person-centered care: The business Case. Scan Foundation.

43. Stewart, M., Ryan, B.L., & Bodea, C. (2011). Is patient-centered care
associated with lower diagnostic costs? *Healthcare Policy*, 6(4), 27–31.

44. Terhune, C. (2017). Putting a lid on waste: Needless medical
tests not only cost $200B—they can do harm. California

Healthline. http://californiahealthline.org/news/putting-a-lid-on-waste-needless-medical-tests-not-only-cost-200b-they-can-do-harm/?utm_campaign=KHN%3A%20 First%20 Edition&utm_source=hs_email&utm_medium=email&utm_content=52143508&_hsenc=p2ANqtz-9fHx6id5bgg12UIoaK7uuug_Vr1QdNRtusHwQDkvEPpDUrna38J6bDCWNlgdfOn_qmBpusggBz4wNfhhQRYPbYQbfIxA&_hsmi=52143508. Accessed May 2017.

45. Gerhardt,W.,Korenda,L.,Mitchell,M.,&Vadnerkar,G.(2015).The road to value-based care. Your mileage may vary. https://dupress.deloitte.com/ content/dam/dup-us-en/articles/value-based-care-market-shift/DUP1063_Value-based-care_vFINAL_5.11.15.pdf. Accessed March 2017.

46. McDonald, P.A., Mecklenburg, R., & Martin, L.A. (2015). The employer-led health care revolution. *Harvard Business Review*. https://hbr.org/2015/07/ the-employer-led-health-care-revolution. Accessed March 2017.

47. Slotkin, J.R., Ross, O.A., Coleman, M.R., & Ryu, J. (2017). Why GE, Boeing, Lowe's, and Walmart are directly buying health care for employees. *Harvard Business Review*. https://hbr.org/2017/06/why-ge-boeinglowes-and-walmart-are-directly-buying-health-care-for-employees. Accessed June 2017.

48. https://www.advisory.com/daily-briefing/2016/12/21/cms-launches-two-new-mandatory-bundled-payment-models. Accessed March 2017.

Chapter 3

1. Bipartisan Policy Center (2014). America's long-term care crisis: Challenges in financing and delivery. https://bipartisanpolicy.org/library/americas-long-term-care-crisis/. Accessed April 2017.

2. Activities of daily living include: toileting, bathing, dressing, eating, transferring out of bed, incontinence care, meal preparation, housekeeping, and medication management.

3. Bipartisan Policy Center (2014). America's long-term care crisis: Challenges in financing and delivery. https://bipartisanpolicy.org/library/americas-long-term-care-crisis/. Accessed April 2017.

4. US Department of Health and Human Services. https://longtermcare. acl.gov/the-basics/. Accessed April 2017.

5. Ramnarace, C. (2011). 10 misconceptions about long-term care insurance. AARP Medicare Resource Center. http://www.aarp.org/ health/ medicare-insurance/info-10-2011/long-term-care-insurance-misconceptions.html. Accessed April 2017.

6. The Scan Foundation. http://www.thescanfoundation.org/publications? keys=&field_article_categories_tid=All&field_series_tid=512. Accessed April 2017.

7. Bipartisan Policy Center (2014). America's long-term care crisis: Challenges in financing and delivery. https://bipartisanpolicy.org/library/americas-long-term-care-crisis/. Accessed April 2017.

8. People born between 1946 and 1964.

9. Bipartisan Policy Center (2014). America's long-term care crisis: Challenges in financing and delivery. https://bipartisanpolicy.org/library/americas-long-term-care-crisis/. Accessed April 2017.

10. OECD. Public spending on health and long-term care: a new set of projections. http://www.oecd.org/eco/growth/public-spending-on-health-and-long-term-care.htm. Accessed April 2017.

11. World Health Organization. Ageing and life-course. Long-term care systems. http://www.who.int/ageing/long-term-care/en/. Accessed April 2017.

12. Gibson, M.J., Gregory, S.R., & Pandya, S.M. (2003). Long-term care in developed nations: A brief overview. AARP. http://assets.aarp.org/rgcen-ter/health/2003_13_ltc_dv.pdf. Accessed April 2017.

13. Wiener, J. (2017). Long-term care financing reform: Can we get there from here? https://www.linkedin.com/pulse/long-term-care- financing-reform-can-we-get-from-here-joshua-wiener. Accessed April 2017.

14. http://www.urban.org/policy-centers/cross-center-initiatives/program-retirement-policy. Accessed April 2017.

15. American Association for Long-Term Care Insurance. How much does

long-term care insurance cost? http://www.aaltci.org/long-term-care-insurance/learning-center/how-much-does-long-term-care-insurance-cost.php. Accessed April 2017.

16. Genworth. Compare long-term care costs across the United States. https://www.genworth.com/about-us/industry-expertise/cost-of-care.html. Accessed April 2017.

17. Ramnarace, C. (2011). 10 misconceptions about long-term care insurance. AARP Medicare Resource Center. http://www.aarp.org/health/medicare-insurance/info-10-2011/long-term-care-insurance-misconceptions.html. Accessed April 2017.

18. Cubanski, J., Casillas, G., & Damico, A. (2015). Poverty among seniors: An updated analysis of national and state level poverty rates under the official and supplemental poverty measures. Kaiser Family Foundation.

19. Interventions that provide temporary breaks for the caregivers that are meant to ensure that the caregiver will be able to maintain care responsibilities.

Chapter 4

1. Alzheimer's Disease International (2013). World Alzheimer Report 2013 reveals global Alzheimer's epidemic creating shortage of caregivers, lack of support from family members. https://www.alz.co.uk/ media/130919. Accessed April 2019.

2. Harris-Kojetin, L., Sengupta, M., Park-Lee, E., Valverde, R., Caffrey, C., Rome, V., & Lendon, J. (2016). Long-term care providers and services users in the US: Data from the national study of long-term care providers, 2013–2014. National Center for Health Statistics. Vital and Health Statistics, 3(38).

3. McAllister, A. & Beaty, J.A. (2016). Aging well: Promoting person-directed care. *Journal of Aging Science*, 4(164), https://doi.org/10.4172/2329–8847.1000164.

4. Ibid.

5. http://www.independent.co.uk/arts-entertainment/obituary-professor-thomaskitwood-1045269.html. Accessed January 2017.

6. Rickert, J. (2012) Patient-centered care: What it means and how to get there. *Health Affairs Blog.* January 24.

7. http://www.thegreenhouseproject.org/. Accessed April 2016.

8. https://drbillthomas.org/about/. Accessed April 2016.

9. http://www.thegreenhouseproject.org/solutions/justify-green-house. Accessed March 2017.

10. Magan, G. (2016). What's so great about culture change? Study offers some clues. LeadingAge. https://www.leadingage.org/cfar/whatsso-great-aboutculture-change-study-offers-some-clues. Accessed March 2017.

11. http://ltcrevolution.com. Accessed March 2017.

12. http://ltcrevolution.com/segments/signature-hometown. Accessed March 2017.

13. McAllister, A. & Beaty, J.A. (2016). Aging well: Promoting person-directed care. *Journal of Aging Science*, 4, 164. https://doi.org/10.4172/2329-8847.1000164.

14. https://www.cms.gov/medicare/provider-enrollment-and-certification/certificationandcomplianc/fsqrs.html. Accessed March 2017.

15. http://www.edenalt.org/international/. Accessed April 2017

16. https://www.youtube.com/watch?v=cr3WuZ1HJHQ.

17. Charras, K & Frémontier, M. (2010) Sharing meals with institutionalized people with dementia: A natural experiment. *Journal of Gerontological Social Work*, 53(5), 436–448.

18. Charras K. & Gzil, F. (2013) Judging a book by its cover: Uniforms and quality of life in special care units for people with dementia. *American Journal of Alzheimer's Disease and Other Dementias*, 28(5), 450–8.

19. Mitchell, G. (2018) Uniforms in dementia care: A barrier or a necessity? *Nursing Ethics*, 25(3) 410–412. https://doi.org/10.1177/0969733015626713.

20. Richardson, M. (2013). The symbolism and myth surrounding nurses' uniform. *British Journal of Nursing*, 8(3) 169–175. http://www.

magonlinelibrary.com/doi/10.12968/bjon.1999.8.3.6704. Accessed March 2017.

21. Alzheimer's Disease International. (2013). World Alzheimer Report 2013 reveals global shortage of caregivers. https://www.alz.co.uk/media/130919. Accessed April 2019.

22. Stanford School of Medicine. https://palliative.stanford.edu/home-hospicehome-care-of-the-dying-patient/where-do-americans-die/. Accessed March 2017.

23. De Roo, M.L., Miccinesi, G., Onwuteaka-Philipsen, B.D., Van Den Noortgate, N., Van den Block, L., Bonacchi, A., Donker, G.A., Lozano Alonso, J.E., Moreels, S., Deliens, L., & Francke, A. L. (2014). Actual and preferred place of death of home-dwelling patients in four European countries: Making sense of quality indicators. *PLOS One*, 9(4). https://doi.org/10.1371/journal.pone.0093762.

24. MedlinePlus. Advance care directives. US National Library of Medicine. https://medlineplus.gov/ency/patientinstructions/000472.htm. Accessed March 2017.

25. Friedman, R.A. (2012). A call for caution on antipsychotic drugs. *The New York Times*. http://www.nytimes.com/2012/09/25/health/a-callfor-caution-in-the-use-ofantipsychotic-drugs.html. Accessed March 2017.

26. Centers for Medicare and Medicaid Services (2014). National Partnership to Improve Dementia Care exceeds goal to reduce use of antipsychotic medications in nursing homes: CMS announces new goal. CMS.Gov. https://www.cms.gov/Newsroom/MediaReleaseDatabase/Press-releases/2014Press-releases-items/2014-09-19.html. Accessed March 2017.

27. World Health Organization (2017). Global action plan on the public health response to dementia 2017–2025. Pg. 5.

28. http://teepasnow.com/. Accessed June 2017.

29. http://www.edenalt.org/events-and-offerings/educational-offerings/dementia-beyond-drugs/. Accessed March 2017.

30. http://www.alpower.net/alpower_Dementia_Beyond_Drugs.htm. Accessed March 2017.

31. http://www.alpower.net/alpower_Dementia_Beyond_Disease.htm. Accessed March 2017.

32. http://schlegelvillages.com/about-us. Accessed March 2017.

33. https://changingaging.org/tag/the-hidden-restraint/. Accessed January 2017.

34. https://changingaging.org/dementia/the-hidden-restraint-part-3/ Accessed June 2017.

35. Eaton, L. (2008). MPs call for better safeguards on antipsychotic use in care homes. *British Medical Journal*, 336(7651), 983.

36. Lindsey, P.L. (2009). Psychotropic medication use among older adults: What all nurses need to know. *Journal of Gerontological Nursing*, 35(9), 28–38.

37. Capezuti, E., Maislin, G., Strumpf, N., & Evans, L.K. (2002). Side rail use and bed-related fall outcomes among nursing home residents. *Journal of American Geriatric Society*, 50(1), 90–6.

38. Neufeld, R.R., Libow, L.S., Foley, W.J., Dunbar, J.M., Cohen, C. & Breuer, B. (1999). Restraint reduction reduces serious injuries among nursing home residents. *Journal of American Geriatric Society*, 47(10), 1202–7.

39. Bowcott, O. (2009). Chemical restraints killing dementia patients. *The Guardian*. https://www.theguardian.com/society/2009/nov/12/anti-psychotic-drugs-killdementia-patients. Accessed March 2017.

40. https://arcare.com.au/dedicated-staff-assignment/. Accessed March 2017.

41. http://www.beatitudescampus.org. Accessed March 2017.

42. http://www.comfortmatters.org. Accessed March 2017.

43. Wyatt, A. (2015). Bringing comfort to people with advanced dementia. Virginia Center on Aging and Virginia Department for Aging and Rehabilitative Services. Vol.3, #3. http://www.sahp.vcu.edu/media/school-of-allied-healthprofessions/virginia-center-on-aging/pdf/ageaction/agesummer15.pdf. Accessed March 2017.

44. http://www.horizonhouse.org/comfort-matters-at-horizon-house/. Accessed March 2017.

Chapter 5

1. Butler, R. (1987). The longevity revolution. *Mt. Sinai Journal of Medicine.* 54(1).

2. Gómez-Batiste, X., Murray, S.A., Thomas, K., Blay, C., Boyd, K., Moine, S. et al.(2016). Comprehensive and integrated palliative care for people with advanced chronic conditions: An update from several European initiatives and recommendations for policy. *Journal of Pain and Symptom Management.* 53(3):509–517.

3. Stjernswärd,J.,Foley,K.M.,&Ferris,F.D.(2007).The public health strategy for palliative care. *Journal of Pain and Symptom Management,* 33(5), 486–493.

4. World Health Organization (2015). Palliative care. http://www.who.int/ mediacentre/factsheets/fs402/en/. Accessed April 2015.

5. The Lewin Group (2010). Individuals living in the community with chronic conditions and functional limitations: A closer look. https://aspe. hhs.gov/system/files/pdf/75961/closerlook.pdf. Accessed April 2017.

6. Kelley, A.S. & Meier, D.E. (2015). The role of palliative care in accountable care organizations. *AJMC.* http://www.ajmc.com/journals/ evidence-based-oncology/2015/april-2015/the-role-of-palliative-care-in-accountable-care-organizations-/P-1. Accessed April 2017.

7. PBS News Hour-Global and regional models for long-term care: Can they work nationally? Solutions for aging with dignity, independence and choice. http://www.thescanfoundation.org/pbs-newshour-global-and-regional-models-long-term-care-can-they-work-nationally-0.19:09. Accessed April 2017.

8. Smith, G., Bernacki, R.B., & Block S.D. (2015). The role of palliative care in population management and accountable care organizations. *Journal of Palliative Medicine,* 18(6), 486–494.

9. Meier, D.E. (2011). Increased access to palliative care and hospice services: Opportunities to improve value in health care. *Milbank Quarterly,* 89(3), 343–380.

10. Gawande, A. (2015). Overkill. An avalanche of unnecessary care is harming patients physically and financially. What can we do

about it? *The New Yorker*. May 11. http://www.newyorker.com/magazine/2015/05/11/overkill-atul-gawande. Accessed April 2017.

11. Makary, M.A. & Daniel, M. (2016). Medical error—The third leading cause of death in the US. *British Medical Journal*. 353: i2139.

12. Kodjak, A. (2016). Dying in a hospital means more procedures, tests, and costs. National Public Radio. http://www.npr.org/sections/health-shots/2016/06/15/481992191/dying-in-a-hospital-means-more-procedures-tests-and-costs. Accessed April 2017.

13. Field, M.J. & Cassel, C.K. (1997). Approaching death: Improving care at the end of life. Institute of Medicine, *National Academy Press*, Washington, D.C.

14. http://www.nationalacademies.org/hmd/Reports/2014/Dying-In-America-Improving-Quality-and-Honoring-Individual-Preferences-Near-the-End-of-Life.aspx. Accessed April 2017.

15. http://atulgawande.com/about/. Accessed April 2017.

16. Ariadne Labs, 2016. https://www.ariadnelabs.org/2016/06/23/read-dr-atul-gawandes-testimony-before-u-s-senate-special-committee-aging-on-serious-illness/. Accessed April 2017.

17. Ibid.

18. Institute of Medicine (2014). Committee on Approaching Death; Addressing key end-of-life issues. Dying in America: Improving quality and honoring individual preferences near the end of life. *National Academy Press*.

19. Parikh, R.B., Kirch, R.A., Smith, T.J., & Temel, J.S. (2013). Early specialty palliative care – Translating data in oncology into practice. *New England Journal of Medicine*, 369(24), 2347–51.

20. https://www.capc.org. Accessed April 2017.

21. National Hospice and Palliative Care Organization. (2015). NHPCO's Facts and Figures. Hospice in America. Pg. 5. https://www.nhpco.org/sites/default/files/public/Statistics_Research/2015_Facts_Figures.pdf. Accessed May 2017.

22. https://www.nytimes.com/2014/09/26/nyregion/family-fights-health-care-system-for-simple-request-to-die-at-home.html?_r=0. Accessed April 2017.

23. http://medicine.hofstra.edu. Accessed April 2017.

24. https://innovation.cms.gov/initiatives/independence-at-home/. Accessed April 2017.

25. https://www.cms.gov/newsroom/mediareleasedatabase/press-releases/2015-press-releases-items/2015-06-18.html. Accessed April 2017.

26. https://www.cms.gov/Newsroom/MediaReleaseDatabase/Pressreleases/2016-Press-releases-items/2016-08-09.htrnon, C.&ml. Accessed April 2017.

27. https://www.northwell.edu/about/news/press-releases/medical-house-calls-program-improves-care-lowers-costs-treating-frail. Accessed April 2017.

28. Activities of daily living include: toileting, bathing, dressing, eating, transferring out of bed, incontinence care, meal preparation, housekeeping, and medication management.

29. https://www.markey.senate.gov//news/press-releases/senators-markeycornyn-bennet-and-portman-introduce-bipartisan-legislation-to-makeinnovative-home-based-primary-care-medicare-program-permanent. Accessed April 2017.

30. https://www.markey.senate.gov//imo/media/doc/2016-07-06-MarkeyIAH-BillText.pdf. Accessed April 2017.

31. Farber, N., Shinkle, D, & Lynott, J., (2011). Aging in place: A state survey of livability policies and practices. AARP Public Policy Institute and National Conference of State Legislatures Research. Report number 2011–13. https://assets.aarp.org/rgcenter/ppi/liv-com/aging-in-place2011-full.pdf. Accessed April 2017.

32. https://blissconnect.com/bliss/. Accessed April 2017.

33. Whitbourne, S.K. (2013). The joys of generativity in midlife. *Huffington Post.* http://www.huffingtonpost.com/susan-krauss-whitbourne/generativity_b_2575916.html. Accessed April 2017.

34. Parikh, R.B., Kirch, R.A., Smith, T.J. & Temel, J.S. (2013). Early specialty palliative care--Translating data in oncology into practice. *New England Journal of Medicine*, 369(24), 2347–51.

Chapter 6

1. WHO (2014). A universal truth: No health without a workforce. http://
    www.who.int/workforcealliance/knowledge/resources/GHWA-a_
    universal_truth_report.pdf?ua=1. Accessed April 2017.

2. Fodeman, J. & Factor, P. (2015). Solutions to the primary care physician
    shortage. *American Journal of Medicine*, 128(8), 800–801.

3. Dall, T., West, T., Chakrabarti, R., & Lacobucci, W. (2014). The
    complexities of physician supply and demand 2016 Update: Projections
    from 2014 to 2025. IHS. https://www.aamc.org/download/426248/ data/
    thecomplexitiesofphysiciansupplyanddemandprojectionsfrom 2013to2.
    pdf. Accessed April 2017.

4. Peterson, S.M., Liaw, W.R., Phillips, R.L., Rabin, D.L., Meyers, D.S., &
    Bazemore, A.W. Projecting US primary care physician workforce needs:
    2010–2025. *Annals of Family Medicine*, 10(6), 503–509.

5. Health Resource Administration (2013). Projecting the supply and
    demand for primary care practitioners through 2020. https://bhw.hrsa.
    gov/health-workforce-analysis/primary-care-2020. Accessed April 2017.

6. Bodenheimer, T. (2008). Coordinating Care—A perilous journey
    through the health care system. *The New England Journal of Medicine*,
    358 (10), 1064–71.

7. Taylor, E.F., Genevro, J., Peikes, D., Geonnotti, K., Wang, W., &
    Meyers, D. (2013)Building quality improvement capacity in primary
    care. Agency for Healthcare Research and Quality. https://www.ahrq.
    gov/professionals/ prevention-chronic-care/improve/capacity-building/
    pcmhqi2.html. Accessed April 2017.

8. (1978). Declaration of Alma-Ata. International Conference on Primary
    Health Care, Alma-Ata, USSR, 6–2. http://www.who.int/publications/
    almaata_declaration_en.pdf. Referenced April, 2017.

9. World Health Organization (1978). Primary Health Care. Report of the
    international conference on primary healthcare. http://apps.who.int/ iris/
    bitstream/10665/39228/1/9241800011.pdf. Accessed April 2017.

10. Donaldson, M.S., Yordy, K.D., Lohr, K.N., & Vanselow, N.A. (1996).
    Primary care. America's health in a new era. Institute of Medicine,

National Academies Press. https://www.nap.edu/read/5152/chapter/1. Accessed April 2017.

11. Martin, J.C., et al. (2004). The future of family medicine: A collaborative project of the family medicine community. *Annals of Family Medicine*. 2(suppl), S3–32. http://www.annfammed.org/content/2/suppl_1/S3. full. Accessed April 2017.

12. Barr, M., Harris, J., Bronson, D.L., Ake, J., Barry, P.P., Cooke, M, Diamond, H.S., Levine, J.S., Mayer, M.E., McGinn, T., McLean, R.M., Starkweather, A.E., & Turton, F.E. (2006). The advanced medical home: A patient-centered, physician-guided model of health care. American College of Physicians. https://www.acponline.org/acp_policy/policies/adv_medicalhome_patient_centered_model_health care_2006.pdf. Accessed April 2017.

13. Nielsen,M.,Langner,B.,Zema,C.,Hacker,T.,& Grundy, P. (2012). Benefits of implementing the primary care patient-centered medical home: A review of cost & quality results, 2012. Patient-Centered Primary Care Collaborative. https://www.pcpcc.org/sites/default/files/media/benefits_ of_implementing_the_primary_care_pcmh.pdf. Accessed April 2017.

14. https://www.pcpcc.org. Accessed April 2017.

15. http://www.ncqa.org/HomePage.aspx. Accessed April 2017.

16. Carret, M., Fassa, A., & Domingues, M. (2009). Inappropriate use of emergency services: A systematic review of prevalence and associated factors. *Cadernos de Saúde Pública*, 25(1), 7–28.

17. Durand, A., Gentile, S., Devictor, B., Palazzolo, S., Vignally, P., Gerbeaux, P., & Sambuc, R. (2011). ED patients: How nonurgent are they Systematic review of the emergency medicine literature. *American Journal of Emergency Medicine*, 29(3), 333–45.

18. Xin, H., Kilgore, M.L., Sen, B.P., & Blackburn, J. (2015). Can nonurgent emergency department care costs be reduced? Empirical evidence from a US nationally representative sample. *Journal of Emergency Medicine*, 49(3), 347–354.

19. High levels of emotional exhaustion and low sense of personal accomplishment.

20. Reid, R.J., Fishman, P.A., Yu, O., Ross, T.R., Tufano, J.T., Soman, M.P., & Larson, E.B. (2009). Patient-centered medical home demonstration: A prospective, quasi-experimental, before and after evaluation. *American Journal of Managed Care*, 15(9), e71–87.

21. Reid, R.J., Coleman, K., Johnson, E.A., Fishman, P.A., Hsu, C., Soman, M.P., Trescott, C.E., Erikson, M. & Larson, E.B. (2010). The Group Health medical home at year two: Cost savings, higher patient satisfaction, and less burnout for providers. *Health Affairs*, 29(5), 835–843.

22. Helfrich, C.D., Dolan, E.D., Simonetti, J., Reid, R.J., Joos, S., Wakefield, B.J., Schectman, G., Stark, R., Fihn, S.D., Harvey, H.B., & Nelson, K. (2014). Elements of team-based care in a patient-centered medical home are associated with lower burnout among VA primary care employees. *Journal of General Internal Medicine*, 29 (Suppl 2), s659–666.

23. http://www.ncqa.org/programs/recognition/practices/pcmh-evidence. Accessed April 2017.

24. http://blog.ncqa.org/ncqa-launches-pcmh-redesign/. Accessed May 2016.

25. Team-based organizational requirements.

26. https://www.bronx.va.gov/. Accessed April 2017.

27. https://www.va.gov/HEALTH/NewsFeatures/2017/March/Robotic-Brace-for-Veterans-of-Spinal-Cord-Injury.asp. Accessed April 2017.

28. Blay, E. Jr., DeLancey, J.O., Hewitt, D.B., Chung, J.W., & Bilimoria, K.Y. (2017). Initial public reporting of quality at Veterans Affairs vs non-veterans affairs hospitals. *JAMA Internal Med*. 177(6) 882–885 https://doi.org/10.1001/jamainternmed.2017.0605.

29. A nephrologist specializes in kidney care.

Chapter 7

1. Value-based reimbursement details can be found in Chap. 1.

2. Bouncebacks are when a patient returns to the ED with the same health issue within 30 days.

3. Blunt, I., Bardsley, M., & Dixon, J. (2010). Trends in emergency admissions in England 2004–2009. Research report. Nuffield Trust.

4. Ostir, G.V., Schenkel, S.M., Berges, I.M., Kostelec, T., & Pimetel, L. (2016). Cognitive health and risk of ED revisit in underserved older adults. *American Journal of Emergency Medicine*, 34(10), 1973–1976.

5. Garland, S.B., (2017). An emergency department designed for older patients. Kiplinger's Retirement Report, February 2017.

6. Erenler, A.K., Akbulut, S., Guzel, M., Cetinkaya, H., Karaca, A., Turkoz, B., & Baydin, A. (2014). Reasons for overcrowding in the emergency department: Experiences and suggestions of an education and research hospital. *Turkish Journal of Emergency Medicine*, 14(2), 59–63.

7. Di Somma, S., Paladino, L., Vaughan, L. Lalle, I., Magnanti, L., Magrini, M. (2015). Overcrowding in emergency department: An international issue. *Internal and Emergency Medicine*. 10(2), 171–175.

8. Boyle, A., Abel, G., Raut, P., Austin, R., Dhakshinamoorthy, V., Ayyamuthu, R., Murdoch, I., & Burton, J. (2015). Comparison of the international crowding measure in emergency departments (ICMED) and the national emergency department overcrowding score (NEDOCS) to measure emergency department crowding: Pilot study. *Emergency Medicine Journal*, 33(5), 307–312.

9. Derlet, R.W. & Richards, J.R. (2002). Emergency department overcrowding in Florida, New York, and Texas. *Southern Medical Journal*, 95(8) 846–849.

10. Derlet, R.W., (2002). Overcrowding in emergency departments: Increased demand and decreased capacity. *Annals of Emergency Medicine*, 39(4), 430–432.

11. Lee, C.C., Lee, N.Y., Chuang, M.C., Chen, P.L., Chang, C.M., & Ko, W.C. (2012). The impact of overcrowding on the bacterial contamination of blood cultures in the ED. *The American Journal of Emergency Medicine*, 30(6), 839–845.

12. Ackroyd-Stolarz, S., Read Guernsey, J., Mackinnon, N.J., & Kovacs, G. (2011). The association between a prolonged stay in the emergency department and adverse events in older patients admitted to hospital: A

retrospective cohort study. *British Medical Journal Quality & Safety*, 20(7). 564–569.

13. Latham, L.P., & Ackroyd-Stolarz, S. (2014). Emergency department utilization by older adults: A descriptive study. *Canadian Geriatrics Journal*, 17(4), 118–125.

14. UN.org. World Population Aging 1950–2050. Chapter IV. http://www.un.org/esa/population/publications/worldageing19502050/. Accessed June 2017.

15. National Institute on Aging. Why population aging matters: A global prospective. Trend 3: Rising numbers of the oldest old. https://www.nia.nih.gov/publication/why-population-aging-matters-global-perspective/trend-3-rising-numbers-oldest-old. Accessed June 2017.

16. Hwang, U., Shah, M.N., Han, J.H., Carpenter, C.R., Siu, A.L., & Adams, J.G. (2013). Transforming emergency care for older adults. *Health Affairs*, 32(12), 2116–2121.

17. US Census Bureau. https://www.census.gov/newsroom/facts-for-features/2015/cb15-ff09.html. Accessed June 2017.

18. Obermeyer, Z., Cohn, B., Wilson, M., Jena, A.B., & Cutler, D.M. (2017). Early death after discharge from emergency department: Analysis of U.S. insurance claims data. BMJ, 356: j239.

19. NEHI(2010).AMatterofurgency:Reducingemergencydepartmentoveruse. http://www.nehi.net/publications/6-a-matter-of-urgency-reducingemergency-department-overuse/view. Accessed June 2017.

20. Uscher-Pines, L., Pines, J., Kellermann, A., Gillen, E., & Mehrotra, A. (2013). Emergency department visits for nonurgent conditions: Systematic literature review. *American Journal of Managed Care*, 19(1), 47–59.

21. Abrashkin, K.A., Washko, J., Zhang, J., Poku, A., Kim, H., & Smith, K.L. (2016) Providing acute care at home: Community paramedics enhance an advanced illness management program—Preliminary data. *Journal of the American Geriatrics Society*, 64(12), 2572–2576.

22. LaMantia, M.A., Lane, K.A., Tu, W., Carnahan, J.L., Messina, F., & Unroe, K.T. (2016). Patterns of emergency department use among long-

stay nursing home residents with differing levels of dementia severity. *Journal of the American Medical Directors Association*, 17(6), 541–546.

23. Burke, R.E., Rooks, S.P., Levy, C., Schwartz, R., & Ginde, A.A. (2015). Identifying potentially preventable emergency department visits by nursing home residents in the United States. *Journal of the American Medical Directors Association*, 16(5), 395–399.

24. Ibid.

25. Weinick, R. M., Burns, R. M., & Mehrotra, A. (2010). Many emergency department visits could be managed at urgent care centers and retail clinics. *Health Affairs*, 29(9), 1630–6.

26. An adverse health event is an unintentional injury incurred because of medical mismanagement or error that results in death, severe illness, hospital admission, lengthened hospital stay, or disability (Szlejf et al., 2012).

27. Han, J.H., Bryce, S.N., Ely, E.W., Kripalani, S., Morandi, A., Shintani, A., Jackson, J.C., Storrow, A.B., Dittus, R.S., & Schnelle, J. (2011). The effect of cognitive impairment on the accuracy of the presenting complaint and discharge instruction comprehension in older emergency department patients. *Annals of Emergency Medicine*, 57(6), 662–671.

28. Martin-Kahn, M., Burkett, E., Schnitker, L., Jones, R.N., & Gray L.C. (2013). Methodology for developing quality indicators for the care of older people in the emergency department. *BMC Emergency Medicine*, 13:23.

29. Gorman, A., (2016). Geriatric ERs reduce stress, medical risks for elderly patients. Kaiser Health News.

30. Ibid.

31. Schnitker, L.M., Martin-Kahn, M., Burkett, E., Beattie, E.R., Gray, L.C. (2013). Appraisal of the quality of care of older adults with cognitive impairment in the emergency department. *Journal of Gerontological Nursing*, 39(3), 34–40.

32. Carpenter, C.R., Bassett, E.R., Fisher, G.M., Shirshekan, J., Galvin, J.E., & Morris, J.C. (2011). Four sensitive screening tools to detect cognitive dysfunction in geriatric emergency department patients: Brief

Alzheimer's screen, Short Blessed Test, Ottawa 3DY, and the caregiver-completed AD8. *Academic Emergency Medicine*, 18(4), 374–384.

33. Hustey, F.M., Meldon, S.W., Smith, M.D., & Lex, C.K. (2003). The effect of mental status screening on the care of elderly emergency department patients. *Annals of Emergency Medicine*, 41(5), 678–684.

34. Lewis, L.M., Miller, D.K., Morley, J.E., Nork, M.J., & Lasater, L.C. (1995). Unrecognized delirium in ED geriatric patients. *The American Journal of Emergency Medicine*, 13(2), 142–145.

35. Han, J.H., Bryce, S.N., Ely, E.W., Kripalani, S., Morandi, A., Shintani, A., Jackson, J.C., Storrow, A.B., Dittus, R.S., & Schnelle, J. (2011). The effect of cognitive impairment on the accuracy of the presenting complaint and discharge instruction comprehension in older emergency department patients. *Annals of Emergency Medicine*, 57(6), 662–671.

36. Ibid.

37. (2013). The geriatric emergency department guidelines. American College of Emergency Physicians, The American Geriatrics Society, Emergency Nurses Association, & the Society for Academic Emergency Medicine. https://www.acep.org/geriedguidelines/. Accessed June 2017.

38. Cubanski, J., & Neuman, T. (2018). The facts on Medicare spending and financing. Kaiser Family Foundation.

39. Moore, B., Levit, K., & Elixhauser A. (2014). Costs for hospital stays in the US, 2012. Agency for Healthcare Research and Quality. https://www. hcup-us.ahrq.gov/reports/statbriefs/sb181-Hospital-Costs-UnitedStates-2012.pdf. Accessed June 2017.

40. Dartmouth Atlas of Health Care, PerryUndem Research & Communication (2013). The revolving door: A report on US Hospital Readmissions. Robert Wood Johnson Foundation. http://www.rwjf.org/en/library/ research/2013/02/the-revolving-door%2D%2Da-report-on-us%2D%2Dhospital-readmissions.html. Accessed June 2017.

41. Ibid.

42. Centers for Disease Control and Prevention. Multiple Chronic Conditions. www.cdc.gov/chronicdisease/about/multiple-chronic.htm. Accessed June 2017.

43. Szlejf, C., Farfel, J.M., Curaiti, J.A., Couto, E. Jr., Jacob-Filho, W., &

Azevedo, R.S. (2012). Medical adverse events in elderly hospitalized patients: A prospective study. *Clinics* (Sao Paulo), 67(11), 1247–1252.

44. Bo, M., Bonetto, M., Bottignole, G., Porrino, P., Coppo, E., Tibaldi, M., Ceci, G., Raspo, S., Cappa, G., & Bellelli, G. (2016). Length of stay in the emergency department and occurrence of delirium in older medical patients. *Journal of the American Geriatrics Society*, 64(5), 1114–1119.

45. Fong, T.G., Tulebaev, S.R., & Inouye, S.K. (2009). Delirium in elderly adults: Diagnosis, prevention and treatment. *Nature Reviews Neurology*, 5(4), 210–220.

46. Ibid.

47. Fong, T.G., Inouye, S.K., & Jones, R.N. (2017). Delirium, dementia, and decline. *JAMA Psychiatry*, 74(3), 212–213.

48. Chodos, A.H., Kushel, M.B., Greysen, S.R., Guzman, D., Kessell, E.R., Sarkar, U., Goldman, L.E., Critchfield, J.M., & Pierluissi, E. (2015). Hospitalization-associated disability in adults admitted to a safety-net hospital. *Journal of General Internal Medicine*, 30(12), 1765–1772.

49. Reichardt, L.A., Aarden, J.J., van Seben, R., van der Schaaf, M., Engelbert, R.H.H., Bosch, J.A., & Buurman, B., M. (2016). Unraveling the potential mechanisms behind hospitalization-associated disability in older patients; the Hospital-Associated Disability and impact on daily life (Hospital-ADL) cohort study protocol. *BMC Geriatrics*, 16(59). https://doi.org/10.1186/s12877-016-0232-3.

50. Covinsky, K.E., Pierluissi, E., & Johnston, C.B. (2011). Hospitalization-associated disability: "She was probably able to ambulate, but I'm not sure." *JAMA*, 306(16), 1782–1793.

51. https://www.fhca.org/members/qi/clinadmin/global.pdf. Accessed June 2017.

52. Fick, D.M., Steis, M.R., Waller, J.L., & Inouye, S.K. (2013). Delirium superimposed on dementia is associated with prolonged length of stay and poor outcomes in hospitalized older adults. *Journal of Hospital Medicine*, 8(9), 500–505.

53. Cole, M.G., Bailey, R., Bonnycastle, M., McCusker, J., Fung, S., Ciampi, A., Belzile, E., & Bai, C. (2015). Partial and no recovery from delirium

in older hospitalized adults: Frequency and Baseline risk factors. *Journal of the American Geriatrics Society*, 63(11), 2340–2348.

54. Iezzoni,L.I.,Dorner,S.C.,&Ajayi,T.(2016).CommunityParamedicine— Addressing Questions as Programs Expand. *The New England Journal of Medicine*, 374, 1107–1109.

55. https://www.dispatchhealth.com. Accessed June 2017.

56. https://www.cms.gov/Medicare/Quality-Initiatives- Patient-AssessmentInstruments/HomeHealthQualityInits/ HHQIHomeHealthStarRatings.html.

57. Becker, M.A., Boaz, T.L., Andel, R., Gum, A.M., & Papadopoulos, A.S. (2010). Predictors of preventable nursing home hospitalizations: The role of mental disorders and dementia. *American Journal of Geriatric Psychiatry*, 18(6), 475–82.

58. Xing, J., Mukamel, D.B., & Temkin-Greener, H. (2013). Hospitalizations of nursing home residents in the last year of life: Nursing home characteristics and variation in potentially avoidable hospitalizations. *Journal of the American Geriatric Society*, 61(11), 1900– 1908. https://doi.org/10.1111/ jgs.12517.

59. Stephens, C.E., Newcomer, R., Blegen, M., Miller, B., & Harrington, C. (2012). Emergency department use by nursing home residents: Effect of severity of cognitive impairment. *The Gerontologist*, 52(3), 383–393.

60. Stephens, C.E., Sackett, N., Govindarajan, P., & Lee, S.J. (2014). Emergency department visits and hospitalizations by tube-fed nursing home residents with varying degrees of cognitive impairment: A national study. *BMC Geriatrics*, 14:35.

61. Givens,J.L., Selby,K.,Goldfeld, K.S.,& Mitchell, S.L.(2012).Hospital transfers of nursing home residents with advanced dementia. *Journal of American Geriatric Society*, 60(5), 905–9.

62. http://www.mountsinai.org/about-us/newsroom/press-releases/ icahnschool-of-medicine-at-mount-sinai-receives-health-care- innovationaward-from-centers-for-medicare-and-medicaid-services. Accessed June 2017.

63. Under a bundled payment agreement, the insurer makes one payment for

the total care linked to a particular procedure or period of time. This fee covers the cost of care across the continuum.

64. Caplan, G.A., Sulaiman, N.S., Mangin, D.A., Aimonino Ricauda, N., Wilson, A.D., & Barclay, L. (2012). A meta-analysis of "hospital in the home." *The Medical Journal of Australia*, 197(9), 512–519.

65. Leff, B., Burton, L., Mader, S.L., Naughton, B., Burl, J., Inouye, S.K., Greenough, W.B.3rd, Guido, S., Langston, C., Frick, K.D., Steinwachs, D., & Burton, J.R. (2005). Hospital at Home: Feasibility and outcomes of a program to provide hospital-level care at home for acutely ill older patients. *Annals of Internal Medicine*, 143(11), 798–808.

66. Single payer is health insurance that is financed by a governmental agency with care delivered by public providers.

67. Managed care organizations function as the insurer, administrator, and provider of health care.

68. https://aspe.hhs.gov/ptac-physician-focused-payment-model-technicaladvisory-committee. Accessed June 2017.

Chapter 8

1. Alzheimer's Disease International (2015). World Alzheimer report 2015: The global impact of dementia. https://www.alz.co.uk/research/WorldAlzheimerReport2015.pdf. Accessed April 2017.

2. Ibid.

3. Ibid.

4. Ibid.

5. Friedman, E.M., Shih, R.A., Langa, K.M., & Hurd, M.D. (2015). US prevalence and predictors of informal caregiving for dementia. *Health Affairs*, 34(10), 1637–1641.

6. Alzheimer's Association, (2017). 2017 Alzheimer's disease facts and figures. http://www.alz.org/facts/. Accessed April 2017.

7. Hurd, M.D., Martorell, P., Delavande, A., Mullen, K.J., & Langa, K.M.

(2013). Monetary costs of dementia in the United States. *New England Journal of Medicine*, 368, 1326–1334.

8. World Health Organization, (2016). Dementia. Fact Sheet. http://www.who.int/mediacentre/factsheets/fs362/en/. Accessed April 2017.

9. World Health Organization, (2012). Dementia. A public health priority. http://apps.who.int/iris/bitstream/10665/75263/1/9789241564458_eng.pdf?ua=1. Accessed April 2017.

10. Alzheimer's Disease International. (2013). World Alzheimer Report 2013 reveals global Alzheimer's epidemic creating shortage of caregivers, lack of support from family members. https://www.alz.co.uk/media/130919. Accessed April 2019.

11. Graham, J. (2014). A shortage of caregivers. *The New York Times*. https://newoldage.blogs.nytimes.com/2014/02/26/a-shortage-of-caregivers/?_r=0. Accessed April 2017.

12. World Health Organization. Supporting in formal caregivers of people living with dementia. http://www.who.int/mental_health/neurology/dementia/dementia_thematicbrief_informal_care.pdf?ua=1. Accessed April 2017.

13. Ibid.

14. Feinberg, L. & Choula, R. Understanding the impact of family caregiving on work. AARP Public Policy Institute. http://www.aarp.org/content/dam/aarp/research/public_policy_institute/ltc/2012/understanding-impact-family-caregiving-work-AARP-ppi-ltc.pdf. Accessed April 2017.

15. Michalowsky, B., Thyrian, J.R., Eichler, T., Hertel, J., Wucherer, D., Flessa, S., & Hoffman, W. (2016). Economic analysis of formal care, informal care, and productivity losses in primary care patients who screened positive for dementia in Germany. *Journal of Alzheimer's Disease*, 50(1), 47–59.

16. Alzheimer's Association, (2017). 2017 Alzheimer's disease facts and figures. http://www.alz.org/facts/. Accessed April 2017.

17. Michalowsky, B., Thyrian, J.R., Eichler, T., Hertel, J., Wucherer, D., Flessa, S., & Hoffman, W. (2016). Economic analysis of formal care, informal care, and productivity losses in primary care patients who

screened positive for dementia in Germany. *Journal of Alzheimer's Disease,* 50(1), 47–59.

18. Reinhard, S.C., Given, B., Huhtala Petlick, N., & Bemis, A. (2008). Supporting family caregivers and providing care. In: Patient safety and quality: An evidence-based handbook for nurses. Rockville (MD): Healthcare Research and Quality (US). Chapter 14. https://www.ncbi. nlm.nih.gov/books/NBK2665/. Accessed April 2017.

19. Zwaanswijk, M., Peeters, J.M., van Beek, A., Meerveld, J., & Francke, A. (2013). Informal caregivers of people with dementia: problems, needs and support in the initial stage and in subsequent stages of dementia: a questionnaire survey. *Open Nursing Journal.* 7, 6–13.

20. Ibid.

21. Alzheimer's Association, (2017). 2017 Alzheimer's disease facts and figures. http://www.alz.org/facts/. Accessed April 2017.

22. (2010). How much is dementia care worth? Lancet Neurology, 9(11), 1037.

23. Vandepitte, S., Van Den Noortgate, N., Putman, K., Verhaeghe. S., Faes, K., & Annemans, L. (2016). Effectiveness of supporting informal caregivers of people with dementia: A systematic review of randomized and non-randomized controlled trials. *Journal of Alzheimer's Disease,* 52(3), 929–65.

24. Mittelman. M.S., Roth, D.L., Clay, O.J., & Haley, W.E. (2007). Preserving health of Alzheimer caregivers: Impact of a spouse caregiver intervention. *American Journal of Geriatric Psychiatry,* 15(9):780–789.

25. Mittelman, M.S., Roth, D.L., Coon, D.W., & Haley, W.E. (2004). Sustained benefit of supportive intervention for depressive symptoms in caregivers of patients with Alzheimer's disease. *American Journal of Psychiatry,* 161(5), 850–856.

26. Mittelman, M.S., Roth, D.L., Haley, W.E., & Zarit, S.H. (2004). Effects of a caregiver intervention on negative caregiver appraisals of behavior problems in patients with Alzheimer's disease: Results of a randomized trial. *The Journals of Gerontology,* Series B, Psychological Sciences and Social Sciences, 59(1), P27–34.

27. Mittelman, M.S., Haley, W.E., Clay, O.J., & Roth, D.L. (2006).

Improving caregiver wellbeing delays nursing home placement of patients with Alzheimer's disease. *Neurology*, 67(9), 1592–1599.

28. Mittelman, M.S., Roth, D.L., Clay, O.J., & Haley, W.E. (2007). Preserving health of Alzheimer's caregivers: Impact of a spouse caregiver intervention. *American Journal of Geriatric Psychiatry*, 15(9), 780–789.

29. Mittelman, M.S. & Bartels, S.J. (2014). Translating research into practice: Case study of a community-based dementia caregiver intervention. *Health Affairs*, 33(4), 587–595.

30. Luchsinger, J.A., Burgio, L., Mittelman, M., Dunner, I., Levine, J.A., Kong, J., Silver, S., Ramirez, M, & Teresi, J.A. (2016). Northern Manhattan Hispanic caregiver intervention effectiveness study: Protocol of a pragmatic randomised trial comparing the effectiveness of two established interventions for informal caregivers of persons with dementia. *BMJ Open*, 6(11), e014082.

31. Gaugler, J.E., Reese, M., & Mittelman, M.S. (2016). Effects of the Minnesota adaptation of the NYU caregiver intervention on primary subjective stress of adult child caregivers of persons with dementia. *The Gerontologist*, 56(3), 461–471.

32. Gaugler, J.E., Reese, M., & Mittelman, M.S. (2015). Effects of the Minnesota adaptation of the NYU caregiver intervention on depressive symptoms and quality of life for adult child care givers of persons with dementia. *American Journal of Geriatric Psychiatry*, 23(11), 1179–1192.

33. Foldes, S.S., & Long K.H. (2014). http://www.actonalz.org/sites/default/files/documents/MN%20Economic%20Model%20of%20Dementia%20White%20Paper%20Final.pdf. Accessed April 2017.

34. https://www.amazon.com/Counseling-Alzheimers-Caregiver-ResourceProfessionals/dp/1579472621.

35. Robbins, L. (2015). With an influx of newcomers, little Chinatowns dot a changing Brooklyn. *The New York Times*. https://www.nytimes.com/2015/04/16/nyregion/influx-of-chinese-immigrants-is-reshapinglarge-parts-of-brooklyn.html?_r=0. Accessed May 2017.

36. Alzheimer's Association. African-Americans and Alzheimer's Disease: The silent epidemic. https://www.alz.org/national/documents/report_africanamericanssilentepidemic.pdf. Accessed May 2017.

37. Alzheimer's Association. African-Americans are at a higher risk for Alzheimer's disease. Accessed May 2017.

38. Kleinfield, N.R. (2016). Fraying at the edges. *The New York Times*. https:// www.nytimes.com/interactive/2016/05/01/nyregion/living-withalzheimers.html?_r=0. Accessed April 2017.

39. Warshaw, G.A., & Bragg, E.J. (2014). Preparing the health care workforce to care for adults with Alzheimer's disease and related dementias. *Health Affairs*, 33(4), 633–41.

40. Henriques, C. (2016). https://alzheimersnewstoday.com/2016/03/31/caregivers-of-people-with-dementia-face-financial-hardships/. Accessed May, 2017.

41. https://www.caringkindnyc.org/_pdf/CaringKind-PalliativeCare Guidelines.pdf. Accessed May 2017.

42. Alzheimer's Association. Wandering and getting lost. http://www.alz. org/norcal/in_my_community_18411.asp. Accessed May 2017.

43. Weeks, L. (2009). Understanding dementia and 'wandering'. The mysteries of dementia-driven wandering. *National Public Radio*.

44. http://www.caringkindnyc.org/wandersafety/. Accessed May 2017.

45. http://daanow.org. Accessed May 2017.

46. http://www.the-ria.ca/walkwithme/livingfully/. Accessed June 2017.

47. Canadian Research Institute for Aging. Accessed June 2017.

48. Batsch, N.L., & Mittelman, M.S. (2012). Overcoming the stigma of dementia. World Alzheimer Report 2012. Alzheimer's Disease International. Pg. 9.

49. Alzheimer's Association (2008). Voices of Alzheimer's disease: A summary report on the nationwide town hall meeting for people with early stage dementia. https://www.alz.org/national/documents/report_townhall.pdf. Accessed May 2017.

50. Batsch, N.L., & Mittelman, M.S. (2012). Overcoming the stigma of dementia. World Alzheimer Report 2012. Alzheimer's Disease International. Pg. 11.

51. Alzheimer's Association (2008). Voices of Alzheimer's disease: A summary report on the nationwide town hall meeting for people with

early stage dementia. https://www.alz.org/national/documents/report_townhall.pdf. Accessed May 2017.

52. Nothing About Us Without Us. Disability Oppression and Empowerment. By James I. Carlton.

53. https://abitofbriansbrilliance.com. Accessed May 2017.

Chapter 9

1. McGinnis, J.M. & Foege, W.H. (1993). Actual causes of death in the United States. *JAMA*, 270(18), 2207–2212.

2. http://www.who.int/about/mission/en/. Accessed October 2017.

3. Healthy life expectancy is defined as the period of life without physical barriers to normal life functioning.

4. McGinnis, J.M., Williams-Russo, P., & Knickman, J.R. (2002). The case for more active policy attention to health promotion. *Health Affairs*, 21(2), 78–93.

5. Please refer to Chap. 8 for more about loneliness interventions and social inclusion.

6. AARP. Waiting for a ride: Transit access and America's aging population. Accessed October 2017.

7. Transportation for America (2011). http://t4america.org/maps-tools/seniorsmobilitycrisis2011/. Accessed October 2017.

8. https://www.ers.usda.gov/topics/food-nutrition-assistance/food-security-in-the-us/. Accessed October 2017.

9. National Council on Aging. https://www.ncoa.org/news/resources-for-reporters/get-the-facts/senior-hunger-facts/. Accessed October 2017.

10. Feeding America. (2017). Senior hunger fact sheet. www.feedingamerica.org/hunger-in-america/senior-hunger-facts.html. Accessed October 2017.

11. Activities of daily living include personal care such as bathing, dressing, grooming, feeding oneself, and toileting.

12. Gundersen, C. & Zillak, J.P., (2015). Food insecurity and health outcomes. *Health Affairs*, 34(11), 1830–1839.

13. Ibid.

14. Malnutrition is defined by the WHO as deficiencies, excesses, or imbalances in a person's intake of energy and/or nutrients resulting in low height and or weight and insufficiencies of micronutrients such as vitamins and minerals. Malnutrition can also cause overweight or obesity, resulting in diseases such as stroke, heart disease, cancer, and diabetes.

15. Vivanti, A.P., McDonald, C.K., Palmer, M.A., & Sinnott, M. (2009). Malnutrition associated with increased risk of frail mechanical falls among older people presenting to an emergency department. *Emergency Medicine Australasia*, 21(5), 386–394.

16. Pereira, G.F., Bulik, C.M., Weaver, M.A., Holland, W.C., & Platts-Mills, T.F. (2015). Malnutrition among cognitively intact, noncritically ill older adults in the emergency department. *Annals of Emergency Medicine*, 65(1), 85–91.

17. Ibid.

18. National Council on Aging. Chronic disease self-management programs. www.ncoa.org/healthy-aging/chronic-disease-self-management-pro-grams/. Accessed October 2017.

19. Ibid.

20. Ahn, S., Basu, R., Smith M.L., Jiang, L., Lorig, K., Whitelaw, N., & Ory, M.G. (2013). The impact of chronic disease self-management programs: Healthcare savings through a community based intervention. *BMC Public Health*, 13, 1141.

21. US Department of Health and Human Services. (2014). Multiple chronic conditions—A strategic framework: Optimum health and quality of life for individuals with multiple chronic conditions. https://www.hhs.gov/sites/default/files/ash/initiatives/mcc/mcc_framework.pdf. Accessed June 2017.

22. Salive, M.E. (2013). Multimorbidity in older adults. *Epidemiologic Reviews*, 35(1), 75–83.

23. Ralph, N.L., Mielenz, T.J., Parton, H., Flatley, A.M., & Thorpe, L.E. (2013). Multiple chronic conditions and limitations in activities of daily living in a community-based sample of older adults in New York City, 2009. *Preventing Chronic Disease*, 10, E199.

24. Tangiisuran, B., Gozzoli, M.P., Davies, J.G. & Rajkumar C. (2010). Adverse drug reactions in older people. *Reviews in Clinical Gerontology*, 20(3), 246–259.

25. Brahma, D.K., Wahlang, J.B., Marak, M.D. & Sangma, M.Ch. (2013). Adverse drug reactions in the elderly. *Journal of Pharmacology and Pharmacotherapeutics*, 4(2), 91–94.

26. Centers for Disease Control. https://www.fda.gov/ForConsumers/ ConsumerUpdates/ucm399834.htm. Accessed October 2017.

27. Tangiisuran, B., Scutt, G., Stevenson, J., Wright, J., Onder, G., Petrovic, M., van der Cammen, T.J., Rajkumar, C., & Davies, G. (2014). Development and validation of a risk model for predicting adverse drug reactions in older people during hospital stay: Brighton Adverse Drug Reactions Risk (BADRI) Model. *PLOS One*, 9(10), e111254.

28. An adverse drug event occurs when a person experiences harm because of a medication.

29. Nair, N.P., Chalmers, L., Peterson, G.M., Bereznicki, B.J., Castelino, R.L., & Bereznicki, L.R. (2016). Hospitalization in older patients due to adverse drug reactions—The need for a prediction tool. *Clinical Interventions in Aging*, 11, 497–505.

30. Pretorius, R.W., Gataric, G., Swedlund, S.K., & Miller, J.R. (2013). Reducing the risk of adverse drug events in older adults. *American Family Physician*, 87(5), 331–336.

31. Thomas, R., Huntley. A.L., Mann, M., Huws, D., Elwyn, G., Paranjothy, S., & Purdy, S. (2014). Pharmacist-led interventions to reduce unplanned admissions for older people: A systematic review and meta-analysis of randomized controlled trials, *Age and Aging*, 43(2), 174–187.

32. Partners in Care Foundation. https://www.picf.org/innovations2/. Accessed October 2017.

33. Pretorius, R.W., Gataric, G., Swedlund, S.K., & Miller, J.R. (2013). Reducing the risk of adverse drug events in older adults. *American Family Physician*, 87(5), 331–336.

34. Andersen, C.K., Wittrup-Jensen, K.U., Lolk, A., Andersen, K., & Kragh-Sørensen, P. (2004). Ability to perform activities of daily living is

the main factor affecting quality of life in patients with dementia. *Health and Quality of Life Outcomes*, 2, 52.

35. CDC. https://www.cdc.gov/pcd/issues/2013/13_0159.htm. Accessed October, 2017.

36. CDC. https://www.cdc.gov/media/releases/2016/p0922-older-adultfalls.html. Accessed October 2017.

37. WHO. http://www.who.int/mediacentre/factsheets/fs344/en/. Accessed October 2017.

38. Ibid.

39. Disability adjusted life year is the years of healthy life lost due to poor health or disability.

40. WHO. http://www.who.int/mediacentre/factsheets/fs344/en/. Accessed October 2017.

41. Isenring, E., Baker, J., & Kerr, G. (2013). Malnutrition and falls risk in community-dwelling older adults. *The Journal of Nutrition, Health, and Aging*, 17(3), 277–279.

42. National Council on Aging. https://www.ncoa.org/news/resources-forreporters/get-the-facts/falls-prevention-facts/. Accessed October 2017.

43. Centers for Disease Control and Prevention. https://www.cdc.gov/homeandrecreationalsafety/falls/adultfalls.html. Accessed October 2017.

44. Ibid.

45. Ibid.

46. Keall, M.D., Pierse, N., Howden-Chapman, P., Guria, J., Cunningham, C.W., & Baker, M.G. (2017). Cost-benefit analysis of fall injuries prevented by a programme of home modifications: A cluster randomized control trial. *Injury Prevention*, 23(1), 22–26.

47. Ibid.

48. https://www.picf.org. Accessed October 2017.

49. http://www.eblcprograms.org. Accessed October 2017

50. On the Medicare Hospital Compare Website, it says: National rate of all cause hospital-wide readmission = 15.3% https://www.medicare.gov/hospitalcompare/profile.html#vwgrph=1&profTab=4&ID=050082&Distn=1.3&dist=50&loc=93030&lat=34.2054029&lng=-119.1681373

According to AHRQ, in 2014 the number was 17.3%. https://www.hcup-us.ahrq.gov/reports/statbriefs/sb230-7-Day-Versus-30-Day-Readmissions.pdf

More info:

In 2003, almost 20 percent of Medicare patients who were discharged from a hospital were readmitted within 30 days. The readmission rates declined from 21.5 percent in 2007 to 17.8 percent in 2015 for targeted conditions (i.e., a set of specific diagnoses measured by Medicare), and from 15.3 to 13.1 percent for non-targeted conditions [36].

51. Center for Health Information and Analysis. (2015). Performance of the Massachusetts health care system series: Focus on provider quality. http:// www.chiamass.gov/assets/Uploads/A-Focus-on-Provider-Quality-Jan-2015. pdf. Accessed October 2017.

52. Not actually a name; our actual readmission reduction programs are called "Care Transition Choices" and HomeMedsPlus.

53. We have no documentation that we enable hospitals to discharge earlier. I've never heard anyone representing a hospital say that, have you?

54. https://www.ncoa.org/resources/program-summary-a-matter-of-balance/. Accessed October 2017.

55. https://www.ncoa.org/resources/program-summary-healthy-ideas/. Accessed October 2017.

56. https://www.cdc.gov/learnmorefeelbetter/programs/depression.htm. Accessed October 2017.

57. https://www.ncoa.org/resources/program-summary-healthy-moves-foraging-well/. Accessed October 2017.

58. http://www.projectenhance.org/enhancewellness.aspx. Accessed October 2017.

59. http://www.projectenhance.org/enhancefitness.aspx. Accessed October 2017.

60. https://www.fitandstrong.org. Accessed October 2017.

61. http://nursing.jhu.edu/faculty_research/research/projects/capable/capable-news.html.

62. https://nursing.jhu.edu/faculty_research/research/projects/capable/index.html.

63. https://nursing.jhu.edu/excellence/aging/center/index.html. Accessed October 2017.

64. Instrumental activities of daily living include preparing meals, house cleaning, managing finances, shopping, using the phone or possibly the computer, medication adherence, and pet care.

65. Generativity is the sharing of wisdom and knowledge to guide the next generations. Psychologist Erik Erikson coined the phrase.

Chapter 10

1. Arslantas, H., Adana, F., Abacigil Ergin, F., Kayar, D. & Acar, G. (2015). Loneliness in elderly people, associated factors and its correlation with quality of life: A field study from Western Turkey. *Iranian Journal of Public Health*, 44(1), 43–50.

2. Tian, Q. (2014). Intergeneration social support affects the subjective well-being of the elderly: Mediator roles of self-esteem and loneliness. *Journal of Health Psychology*, 21(6), 1137–1144.

3. Singh, K. & Srivastava, S.K. (2014). Loneliness and quality of life among elderly people. *Journal of Psychosocial Research*, 9(1), 11–18.

4. Luo, Y., Hawkley, L.C., Waite, L.J., & Cacioppo, J.T. (2012). Loneliness, health, and mortality in old age: A national longitudinal study. *Social Science & Medicine*, 74(6), 907–914.

5. Steptoe, A., Shanker, A., Demakakos, P., & Wardle, J. (2013). Social isolation, loneliness, and all-cause mortality in older men and women. *Proceedings of the National Academy of Sciences of the United States of America*, 110(15), 5797–5801.

6. Perissinotto, C.M., Stijacic Cenzer, I., & Covinsky, K.E. (2012). Loneliness in Older Persons: A predictor of functional decline and death. *Archives of Internal Medicine*, 172(14), 1078–1083.

7. World Health Organization (2002). Active aging. A policy framework. http://www.who.int/ageing/publications/active_ageing/en/. Accessed June 2017.

8. Holt-Lunstad, J., Smith, T.B., Baker, M., Harris, T., & Stephenson,

D. (2015). Loneliness and social isolation as risk factors for mortality a meta-analytic review. *Perspectives on Psychological Science*, 10(2), 227–237.

9. Mushtaq, R., Shoib, S., Shah, T., & Mushtaq, S. (2014). Relationship between loneliness, psychiatric disorders and physical health? A review on the psychological aspects of loneliness. *Journal of Clinical & Diagnostic Research*, 8(9), WE01–WE04.

10. McCall, W.V. & Kintziger, K.W. (2013). Late life depression: A global problem with few resources. *The Psychiatric Clinics of North America*, 36(4), 475–481. https://doi.org/10.1016/j.psc.2013.07.001.

11. Liu, L. Gou, Z., & Zou, J. (2014). Social support mediates loneliness and depression in elderly people. *Journal of Health Psychology*, 21(5), 750–758.

12. Gan, P., Xie, Y., Duan, W., Deng, Q., & Yu, X. (2015). Rumination and loneliness independently predict six-month later depression symptoms among Chinese elderly in nursing homes. *PLOS One*, 10(9), e0137176.

13. Wong, N.M.L., Liu, H.L., Lin, C., Huang, C.M., Wai, Y.Y., Lee, S.H., & Lee, T.M.C. (2016). Loneliness in late-life depression: Structural and functional connectivity during affective processing. *Psychological Medicine*, 46(12), 2485–2499.

14. Alzheimer's Disease International (2012). World Alzheimer's report 2012. Overcoming the stigma of dementia. Pg. 9.

15. Thompson, E.H.Jr. & Weaver, A.J. (2016). Making connections: The legacy of an intergenerational program. *The Gerontologist*, 56(5), 909–918.

16. Grefe, D. (2011). Combating ageism with narrative and intergroup contact: Possibilities of intergenerational connections. *Pastoral Psychology*, 60(1), 99–105.

17. Chippendale, T. & Boltz, M. (2015). Living legends: Effectiveness of a program to enhance sense of purpose and meaning in life among community-dwelling older adults. *The American Journal of Occupational Therapy*, 69(4), 1–11.

18. Boyle, P.A., Barnes, L.L., Buchman, A.S., & Bennett, D.A. (2009). Purpose in life is associated with mortality among community-dwelling older persons. *Psychosomatic Medicine*, 71(5), 574–579.

19. Boyle, P.A., Buchman, A.S., Wilson, R.S., Yu, L., Schneider, J.A., &

Bennett, D.A. (2012). Effect of purpose in life on the relation between Alzheimer disease pathologic changes on cognitive function in advanced age. *Archives of General Psychiatry*, 69(5), 499–505.

20. Davy, J. (2012). Generativity: Contributing to others may enhance well-being. InvestigAge. http://www.investigage.com/2012/04/20/generativity-contributing-to-others-June-enhance-well-being/. Accessed June 2017.

21. Hafner, K (2016). Researchers confront an epidemic of loneliness. *The New York Times*. https://www.nytimes.com/2016/09/06/health/lonlinessaging-healtheffects.html?_r=1. Accessed June 2017.

22. Bodewig, C., & Hirshleifer, S. (2011). Advancing adult learning in Eastern Europe and Central Asia. Discussion paper, No. 1108. World Bank.

23. Holodny, E. (2016). This is a pretty worrying chart for China's demographic future. Business Insider. http://www.businessinsider.com/chinaworking-age-population-already-shrinking-2016-5. Accessed June 2017.

24. Bagri, N.T. (2017). China's seniors are lining up to go back to school. Quartz. https://qz.com/978805/chinas-seniors-are-lining-up-to-go-back-to-college/. Accessed June 2017.

25. Ibid.

26. Yiwen, C. (2017). Universities offer lifelong learning to China's elderly. Sixth Tone. http://www.sixthtone.com/news/1840/universities-offer-life-long-learning-to-chinas-elderly. Accessed June 2017.

27. www.aseniorcitizensguideforcollege.com. Accessed June 2017.

28. Manninen, J., Sgier, I., Fleige, M., Thöne-Geyer, B., Kil, M., Možina, E., Danihelková, H., Mallows, D., Duncan, S., Meriläinen, M., Diez, J., Sava, S., Javrh, P., Vrečer, N., Mihajlovic, D., Kecap, E., Zappaterra, P., Kornilow, A., Ebener, R., & Operti, F. (2014). Benefits of lifelong learning in Europe: Main results of the BeLL-Project. Research report.

29. Fei You Community Services (2012). Lifelong learning among older adults in Singapore.

30. http://www.ohchr.org/EN/ProfessionalInterest/Pages/OlderPersons.aspx. Accessed June 2017.

31. The sharing of wisdom and knowledge to guide the next generations. Psychologist Erik Erikson coined the phrase.

32. http://www.beaconhillvillage.org. Accessed June 2017.

33. http://www.beaconhillvillage.org/content.aspx?page_id=22&club_id=332658&module_id=77064. Accessed June 2017.

34. http://www.beaconhillvillage.org/content.aspx?page_id=2. Accessed June 2017.

35. https://www.genworth.com/about-us/industry-expertise/cost-of-care.html. Accessed June 2017.

36. https://www.seniorhomes.com/p/independent-living-costs/. Accessed June 2017.

37. Groer, A. (2017). Baby boomers join 'aging-at-home villages' for yoga, happy hour, cooking classes and biking. *The Washington Post*. https://www.washingtonpost.com/national/health-science/baby-boomers-join-agingat-home-villages-for-yoga-happy-hour-ladies-night-out-tech-class-andbiking/2017/05/04/7fdf5a78-1a2a-11e7-855e-4824bbb5d748_story.html?utm_term=.e701f9bb255e. Accessed June 2017.

38. www.vtvnetwork.org. Accessed June 2017.

39. http://www.vtvnetwork.org/content.aspx?page_id=1905&club_id=691012. Accessed June 2017.

40. Brick, Y., & Clarfield, A.M. (2007). "JDC-ESHEL," a unique non-governmental organization dedicated to the elderly in Israel. *Archives of Gerontology and Geriatrics*, 44(3), 225–234.

41. Strauss, I.E. (2016). The hot new millennial housing trend is a repeat of the middle ages. *The Atlantic*. https://www.theatlantic.com/business/archive/2016/09/millennial-housing-communal-living-middleages/501467/. Accessed June 2017.

42. www.cohousing.org. Accessed June 2017.

43. http://www.cohousing.org/node/3049. Accessed June 2017.

44. http://participateindesign.org/approach/what//. Accessed June 2017.

45. http://swansmarket.com. Accessed June 2017.

46. Accessed June 2017.

47. https://www.stjohnsliving.org/brickstone/gallery. Accessed June 2017.

48. https://www.stjohnsliving.org/uploads/files//meadows/pdf/MeadowsJune.pdf. Accessed June 2017.

49. http://www.beatitudescampus.org/lifestyle/activities-events/. Accessed June 2017.

50. http://www.beatitudescampus.org. Accessed June 2017.

51. http://www.comfortmatters.org. Accessed June 2017.

52. http://www.lasellvillage.org. Accessed June 2017.

53. http://www.lasell.edu/academics/academic-centers/rosemary-b-fuss-center-for-research-on-aging-and-intergenerational-studies.html. Accessed June 2017.

54. https://www.youtube.com/watch?v=FHHhLD9nSU8. Accessed June 2017.

55. World Health Organization (2007). Global Age-Friendly Cities Guide. http://www.who.int/ageing/age_friendly_cities_guide/en/. Accessed June 2017.

56. http://successfulaging.milkeninstitute.org/Juneors-pledge/bcsa-Juneors-pledge-with-intro-letter.pdf. Accessed June 2017.

57. Kubendran, S., & Soll, L. (2007). Best cities for successful aging 2017. Milken Institute Center for the Future of Aging. http://www.milkeninstitute.org/publications/view/852. Accessed June 2017.

58. http://www.dhealthsummit.org/dont-tell-me-how-to-age/. Accessed June 2017.

59. https://apps.vnsny.org/advantage/whatis.html. Accessed June 2015.

60. https://www.mailman.columbia.edu/research/age-smart-employer. Accessed June 2017.

61. Greenwald, L., Copeland, C., & VanDerhei, J. (2017). The 2017 retirement confidence survey: Many workers lack retirement confidence and feel stressed out about retirement preparations. Employee Benefits Research Institute.

62. Siedle, E. (2013). The greatest retirement crisis in American history. *Forbes*. https://www.forbes.com/sites/edwardsiedle/2013/03/20/the-greatestretirement-crisis-in-american-history/#c14762f55b6f. Accessed June 2017.

63. McGee, S. (2015). New study reminds us that Americans are woefully

unprepared for retirement. *The Guardian*. https://www.theguardian. com/money/2015/jun/07/study-ramericans-retirement-401k-socialsecurity. Accessed June 2017.

64. Kirkham, E. (2016). 1 in 3 Americans has saved $0 for retirement. *Money*. http://money.com/money/4258451/retirement-savings-survey/. Accessed June 2017.

65. Choe, S. (2017). Punching in past 65: Older-worker rate highest since 1962. *The Associated Press*. https://www.usatoday.com/story/money/personalfinance/retirement/2017/05/10/punching-past-65-olderworker-rate-highest-since-1962/101447336/. Accessed June 2017.

66. Oxford Policy & Human Development Initiative. http://www.ophi.org. uk/research/missing-dimensions/social-connectedness/social-isolation/. Accessed June 2017.

67. Butrica, B.A., Smith, K.E., & Steuerle, C.E. (2006). Working for a good retirement. The Retirement Project. The Urban Institute. Pgs. 19–20.

68. Ibid.

69. Carnevale, A.P., Hanson, A.R., & Gulish, A. (2013). Failure to launch. Structural shift and the new lost generation. The Generations Initiative. Georgetown University. Pg. 40.

70. Boston Consulting Group. The global workforce crisis: $10 trillion at risk. https://www.bcgperspectives.com/content/articles/management_two_speed_economy_public_sector_global_workforce_ crisis/?chapter=2. Accessed June 2017.

71. http://agesmartemployer.org. Accessed June 2017.

72. Butler, R.N. (1969). Age-ism: another form of bigotry. *The Gerontologist*, 9(4), 243–246.

73. Richeson, J.A., & Shelton, N. (2006). A social psychological perspective on the stigmatization of older adults. In: National Research Council (US) Committee on Aging Frontiers in Social Psychology, Personality, and Adult Developmental Psychology; Carstensen LL, Hartel CR, editors. When I'm 64. Washington DC, *National Academies Press*.

74. https://www.exceedingexpectations.nyc. Accessed June 2017.

75. https://nyam.org/age-friendly-nyc/. Accessed May 2017.

76. https://nyam.org/media/filer_public/f6/7f/f67fe2c7-f400-4060-8919081766131eda/agefriendlyfindingsreport.pdf. Accessed May 2017.

77. http://www.nyc.gov/html/dfta/downloads/pdf/age_friendly_report13.pdf. Accessed May 2017.

78. https://nyam.org/age-friendly-nyc/resources/tools-publications/tools/. Accessed May 2017.

79. https://network.aia.org/designforaging/home. Accessed May 2017.

80. https://main.aiany.org. Accessed May 2017.

81. http://www.ibasho.org/web/. Accessed June 2017.

82. Harvey, S.A. (2013). Natural disasters are especially hard on seniors. *The Cornell Chronicle*. Cornell University. http://news.cornell.edu/stories/2013/03/natural-disasters-are-especially-hard-seniors. Accessed June 2017.

83. Kulcsar, A. (2013). Older people disproportionately affected by Typhoon Haiyan. HelpAge International. http://www.helpage.org/newsroom/latest-news/older-people-disproportionately-affected-by-typhoon-haiyan/. Accessed June 2017.

84. Parry, W. (2013). Why disasters like Sandy hit the elderly hard. LiveScience. http://www.livescience.com/27752-natural-disasters-hitelderly-hard.html. Accessed June 2017.

85. CDC's Disaster Planning Goal: Protect Vulnerable Older Adults. https:// www.cdc.gov/aging/pdf/disaster_planning_goal.pdf. Accessed June 2017.

86. https://www.youtube.com/watch?v=D8R6VkqvsBY. Accessed June 2017.

87. http://timebanks.org. Accessed June 2017.

88. https://vimeo.com/110908351. Accessed June 2017.

89. http://www.scie.org.uk/publications/guides/guide51/what-is-coproduction/defining-coproduction.asp. Accessed June 2017.

90. https://community.linkages.org. Accessed June 2017.

91. https://innovation.pamf.org. Accessed June 2017.

92. Sederer, Lloyd (2013). Population health: Transforming health care to improve our health. *Huffington Post*. http://www.huffingtonpost.com/lloyd-i-sederer-md/health-care_b_4455582.html. Accessed June 2015.

93. Robert Wood Johnson (2014). http://www.rwjf.org/en/library/collections/super-utilizers.html. Accessed June 2015.

Chapter 11

1. Hafner, K. (2016). As population ages, where are the geriatricians? *The New York Times*. http://www.nytimes.com/2016/01/26/health/where-are-the-geriatricians.html. Accessed April 2017.

About the Authors

William A. Haseltine, PhD

William Haseltine is the Chair and President of ACCESS Health International. He was a professor at Harvard Medical School and Harvard School of Public Health from 1976 to 1993, where he was founder and the chair of two academic research departments, the Division of Biochemical Pharmacology and the Division of Human Retrovirology. He is well known for his pioneering work on cancer, HIV/AIDS, and genomics. He has authored more than 200 manuscripts in peer-reviewed journals and is the author of several books, including *World Class: A Story of Adversity, Transformation, and Success at NYU Langone Health*, *Voices in Dementia Care: Reimagining the Culture of Care*, *Aging with Dignity: Innovation and Challenge in Sweden*, and *Affordable Excellence: The Singapore Healthcare Story*.

Jean Galiana, MASM, RCFE

In her role at ACCESS Health International, Jean Galiana successfully promoted key messages about elder care and optimal aging to engage policy makers, health care providers, the general public, and stakeholders.

She managed qualitative research projects to discover, document, and advocate for best practices in aging in the United States. Currently Jean works in communications and survey research for Vital Research in Los Angeles, CA. She obtained her undergraduate degree in business from Lehman College and holds a master's degree in aging services management from the University of Southern California Leonard Davis School of Gerontology.